FOR ORGANS, PIANOS & ELECTRONIC KEYBOARDS

E-Z PLAY® TODAY

185

CARPENTERS

ISBN 0-634-03239-9

HAL•LEONARD®
CORPORATION

7777 W. BLUEMOUND RD. P.O. BOX 13819 MILWAUKEE, WI 53213

E-Z Play® Today Music Notation © 1975 by HAL LEONARD CORPORATION
E-Z PLAY and EASY ELECTRONIC KEYBOARD MUSIC are registered trademarks of HAL LEONARD CORPORATION.

Visit Hal Leonard Online at
www.halleonard.com

CARPENTERS

CONTENTS

Bless the Beasts and Children

Registration 3
Rhythm: Slow Rock or Ballad

Words and Music by Barry DeVorzon
and Perry Botkin, Jr.

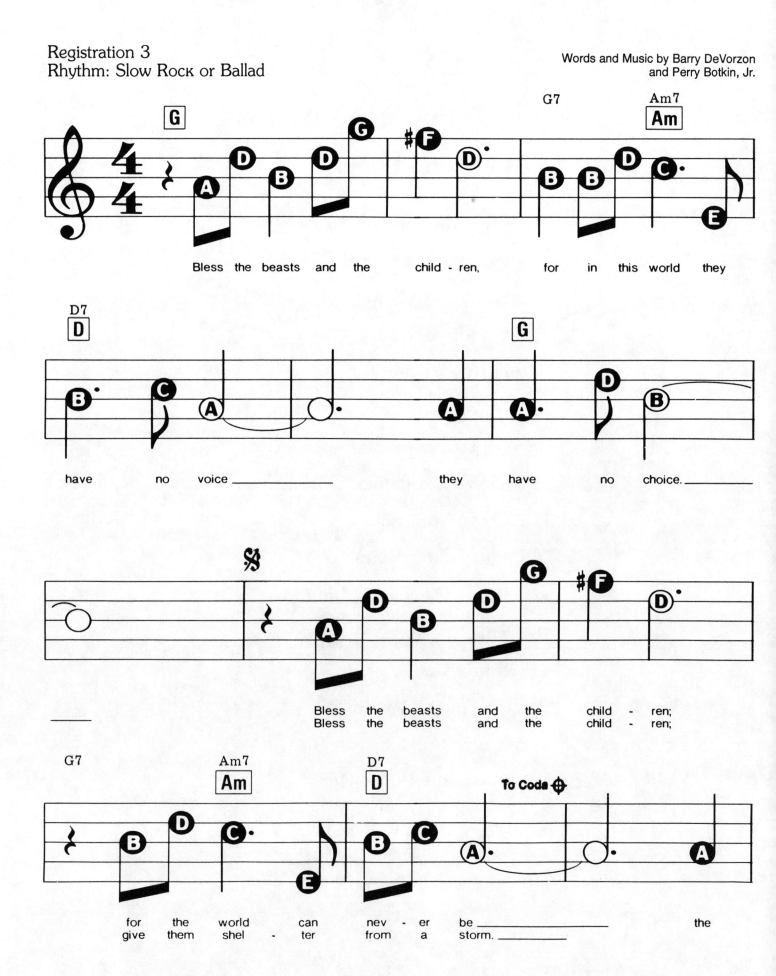

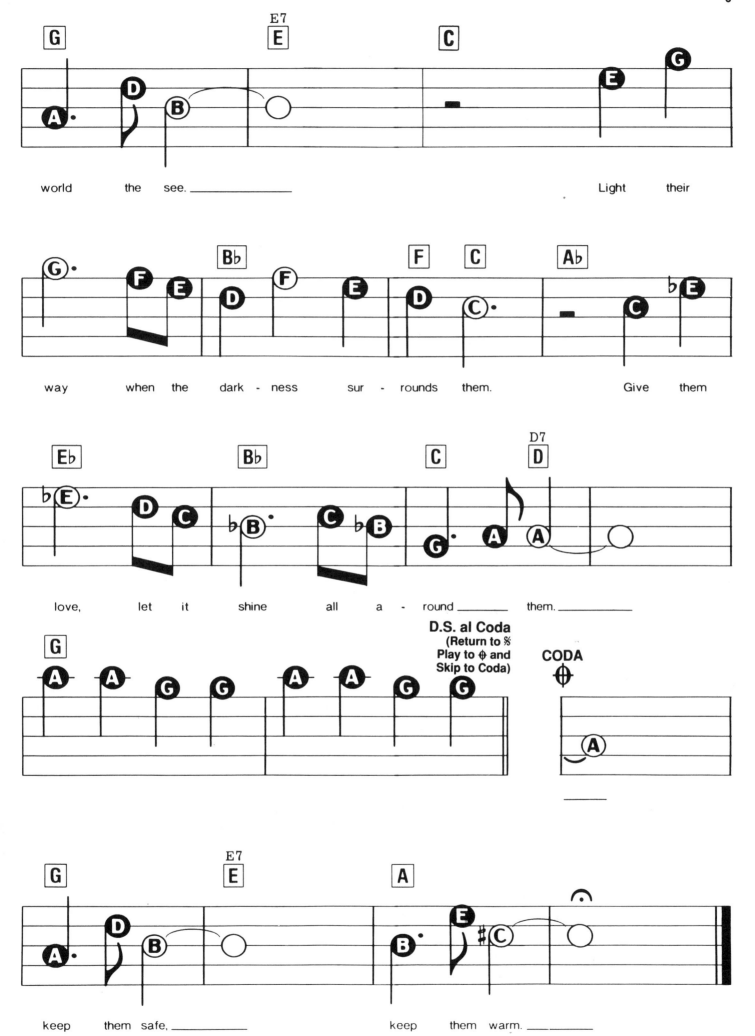

(They Long to Be)
Close to You

Registration 10
Rhythm: Swing, Shuffle, or Ballad

Lyric by Hal David
Music by Burt Bacharach

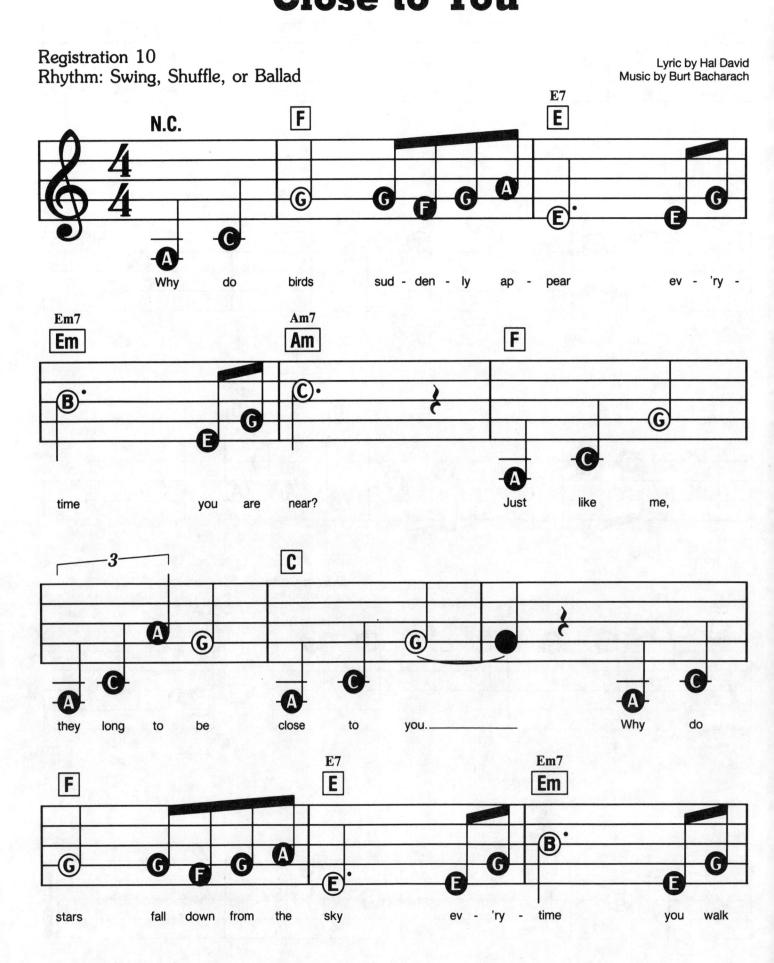

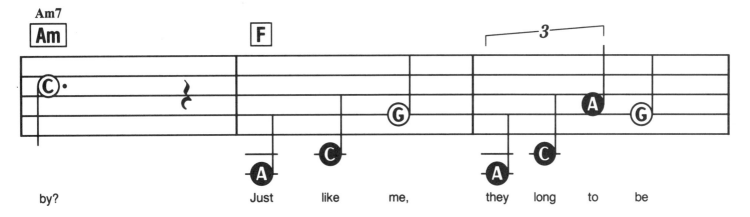

by? Just like me, they long to be

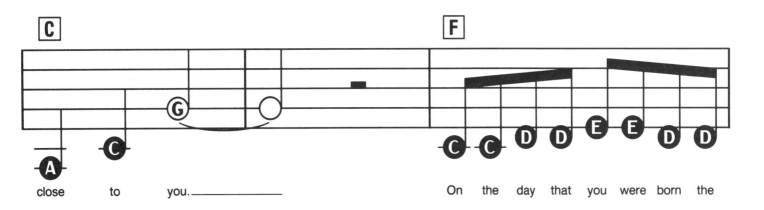

close to you._____ On the day that you were born the

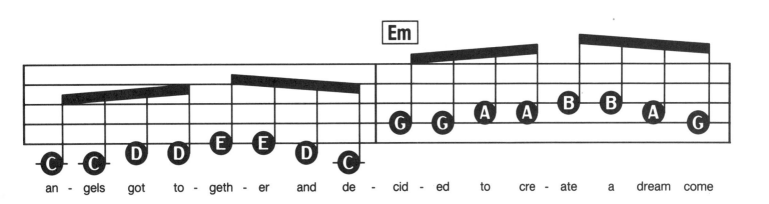

an - gels got to - geth - er and de - cid - ed to cre - ate a dream come

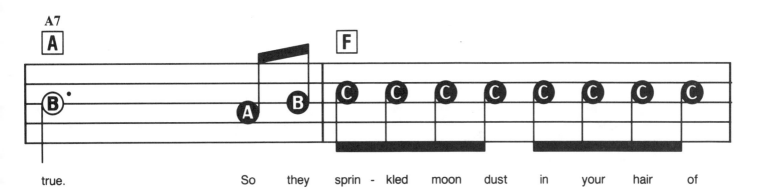

true. So they sprin - kled moon dust in your hair of

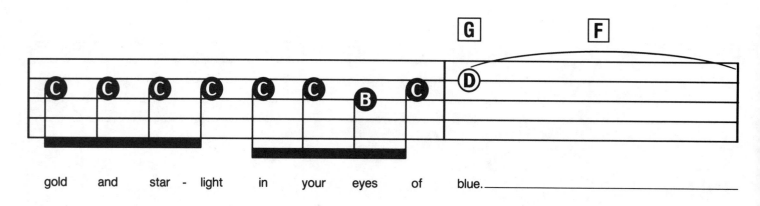

gold and star - light in your eyes of blue.

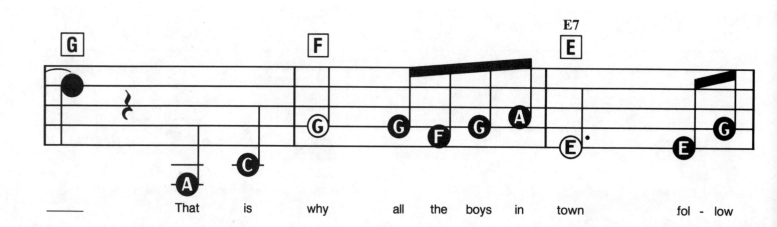

That is why all the boys in town fol - low

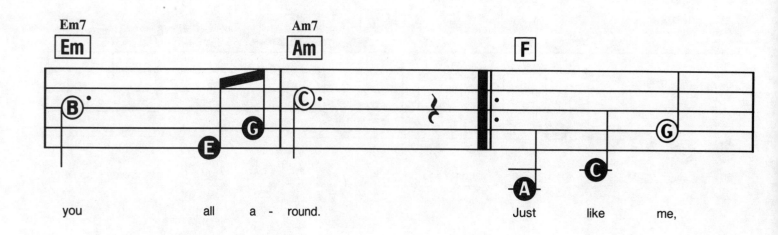

you all a - round. Just like me,

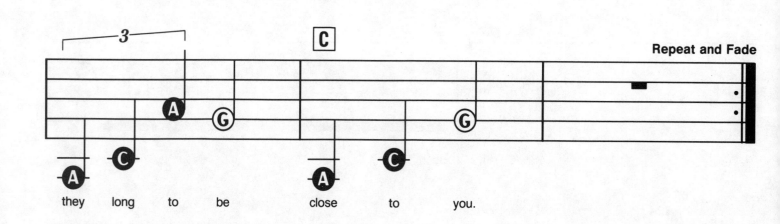

Repeat and Fade

they long to be close to you.

For All We Know
from the Motion Picture LOVERS AND OTHER STRANGERS

Registration 3
Rhythm: Rock or Ballad

Words by Robb Wilson and James Griffin
Music by Fred Karlin

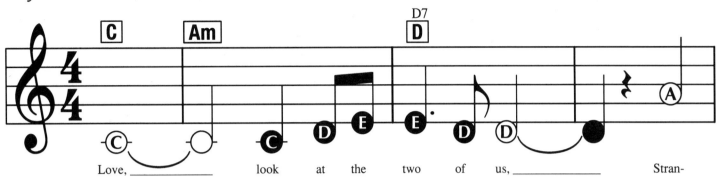

Love, _____ look at the two of us, _____ Stran-

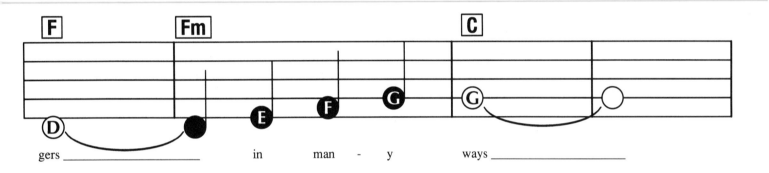

gers _____ in man - y ways _____

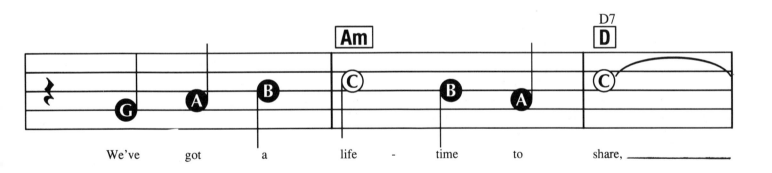

We've got a life - time to share, _____

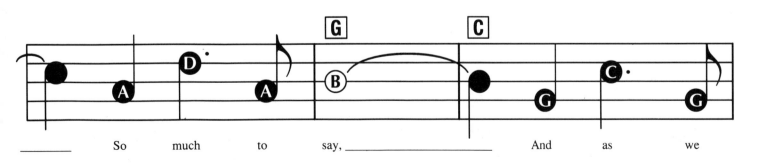

_____ So much to say, _____ And as we

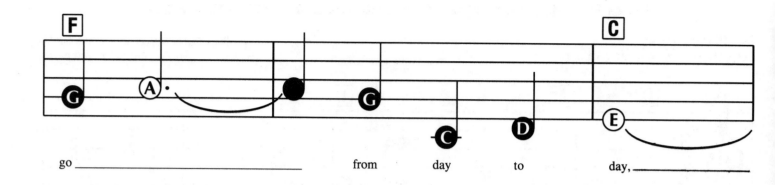

go _____ from day to day, _____

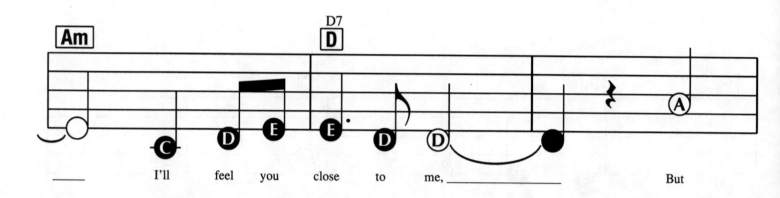

_____ I'll feel you close to me, _____ But

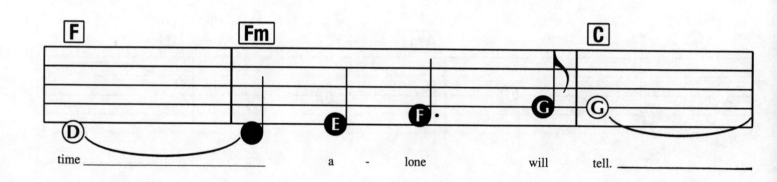

time _____ a - lone will tell. _____

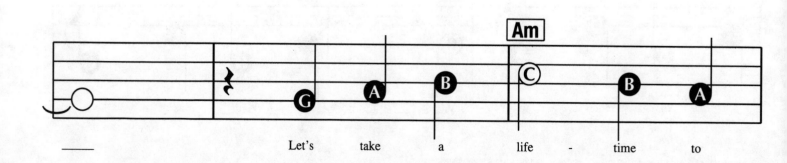

_____ Let's take a life - time to

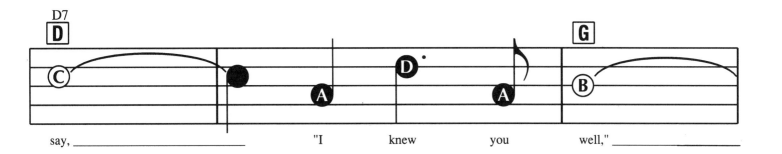

say, _____ "I knew you well," _____

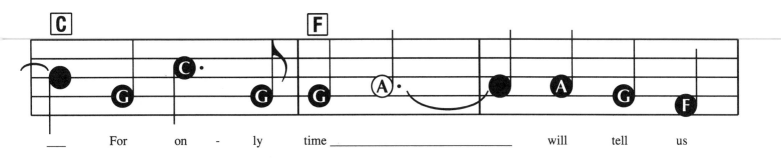

__ For on - ly time _____ will tell us

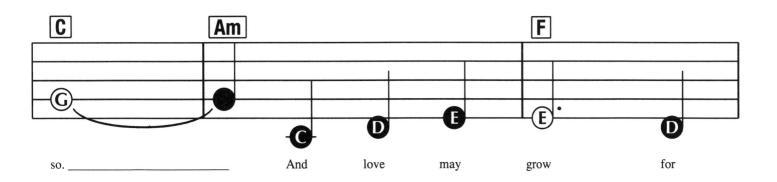

so. _____ And love may grow for

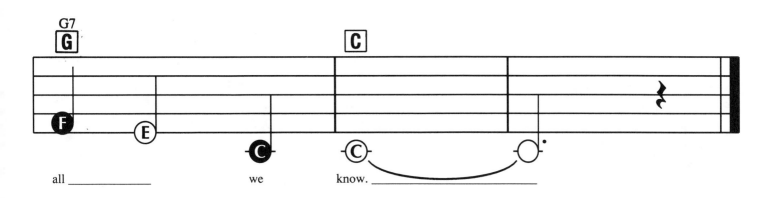

all _____ we know. _____

Goodbye to Love

Registration 8
Rhythm: 8 Beat or Rock

Words and Music by Richard Carpenter
and John Bettis

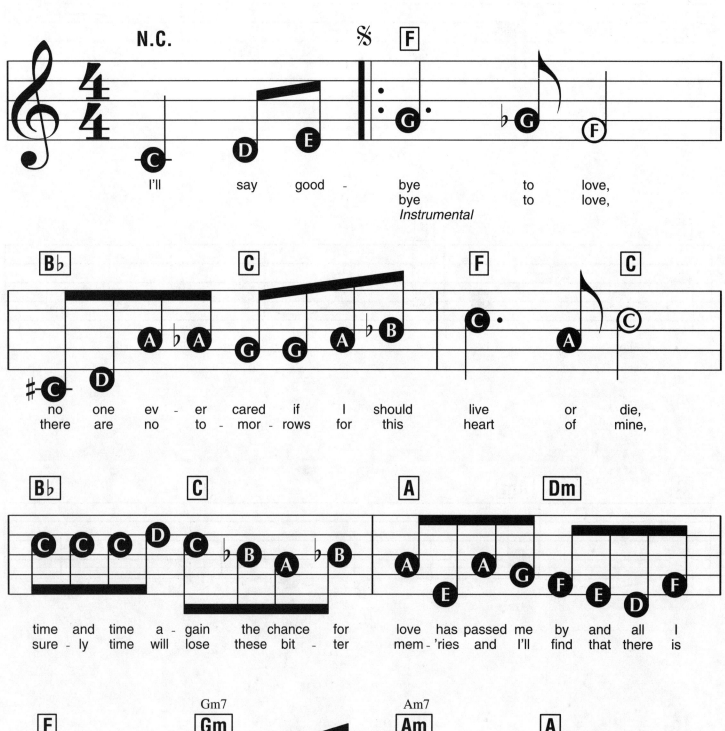

I'll say good - bye to love,
bye to love,
Instrumental

no one ev - er cared if I should live or die,
there are no to - mor - rows for this heart of mine,

time and time a - gain the chance for love has passed me by and all I
sure - ly time will lose these bit - ter mem - 'ries and I'll find that there is

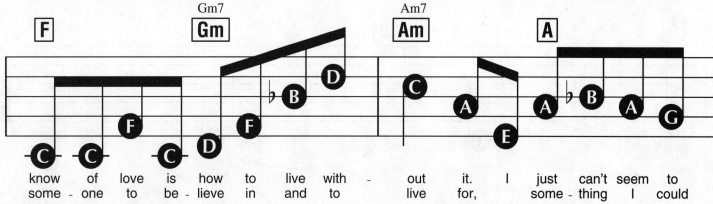

know of love is how to live with - out it. I just can't seem to
some - one to be - lieve in and to live for, some - thing I could

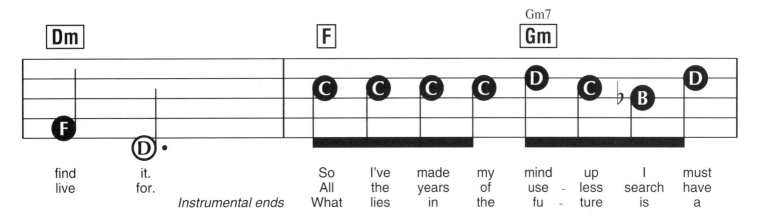

find it. / live it for. *Instrumental ends*

So I've made my mind up I must
All the years of the future is a
What lies in the use - less search have

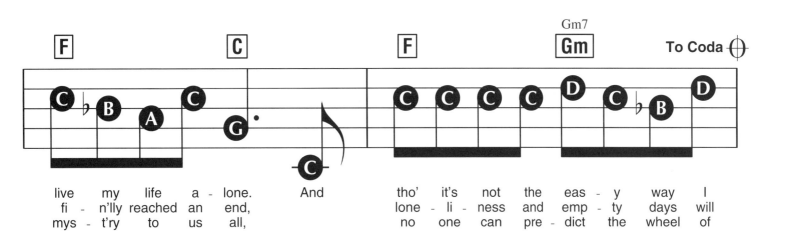

live my life a - lone. And
fi - n'lly reached an end,
mys - t'ry to us all,

tho' it's not the eas - y way I
lone - li - ness and emp - ty days will
no one can pre - dict the wheel of

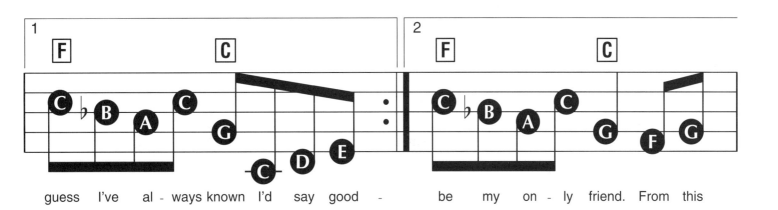

guess I've al - ways known I'd say good -
be my on - ly friend. From this

D.S. al Coda
(Return to 𝄋
Play to ⊕ and
Skip to Coda)

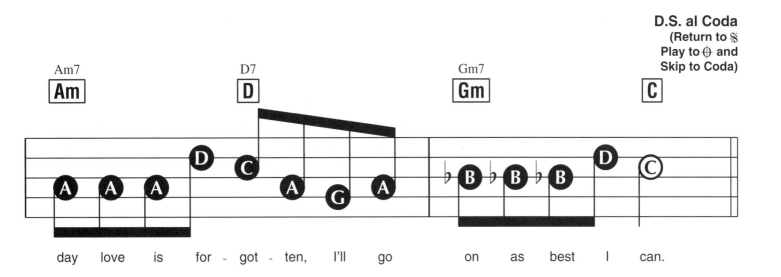

day love is for - got - ten, I'll go on as best I can.

14

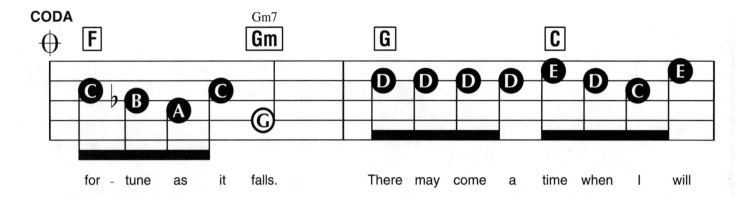

for - tune as it falls.   There may come a time when I will

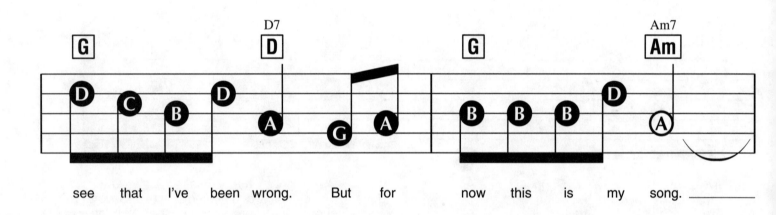

see that I've been wrong.   But for   now this is my song. _____

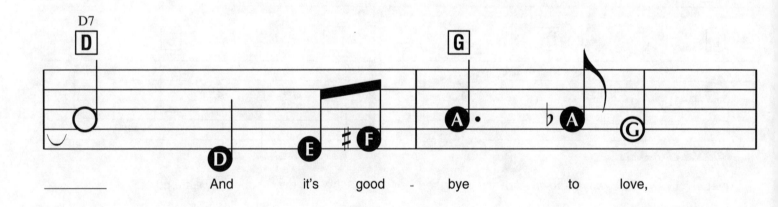

_____   And   it's good - bye   to love,

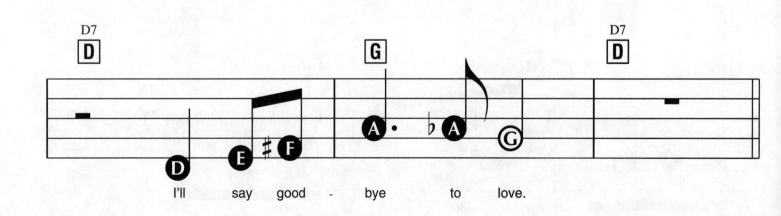

I'll say good - bye   to love.

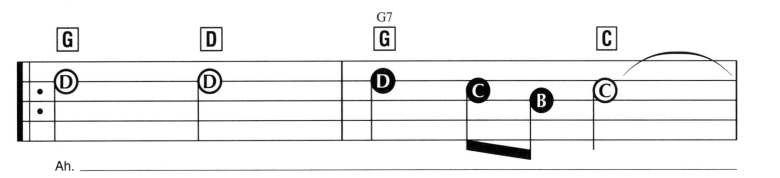

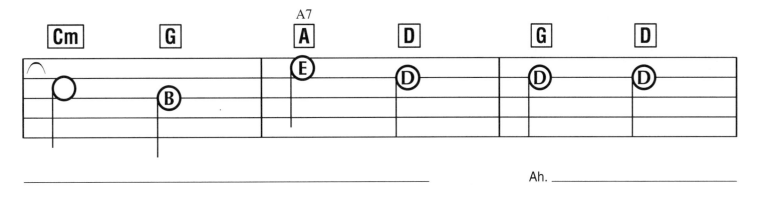

Repeat and Fade

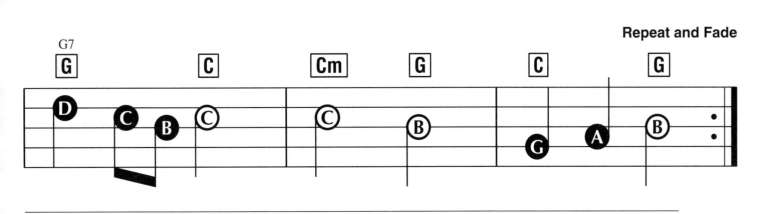

Hurting Each Other

Registration 8
Rhythm: Rock

Words by Peter Udell
Music by Gary Geld

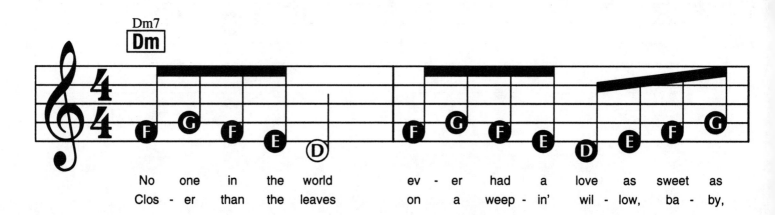

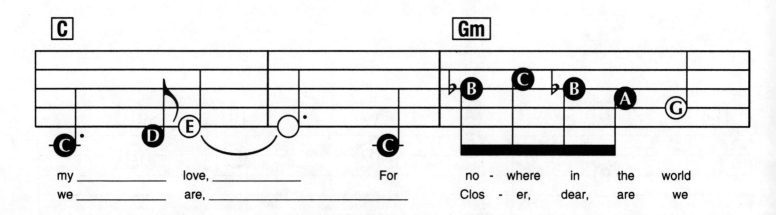

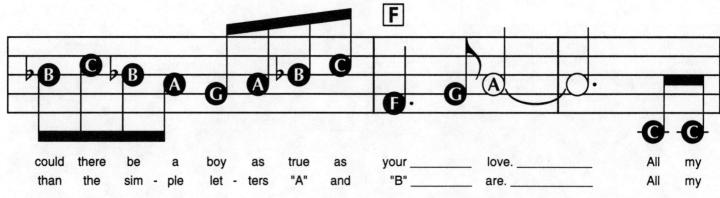

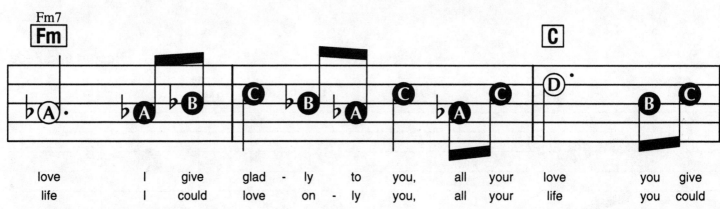

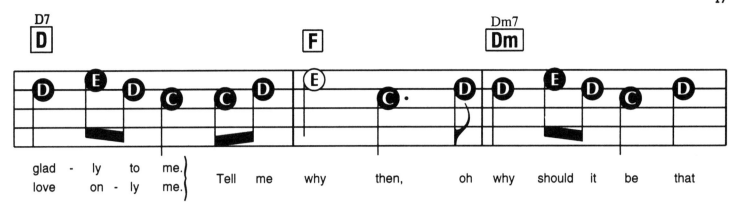

glad - ly to me.
love on - ly me.

Tell me why then, oh why should it be that

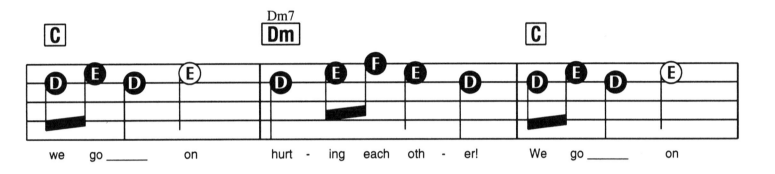

we go _____ on

hurt - ing each oth - er!

We go _____ on

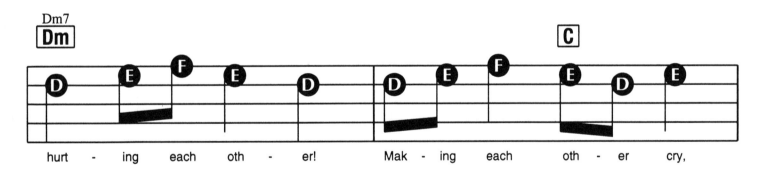

hurt - ing each oth - er!

Mak - ing each oth - er cry,

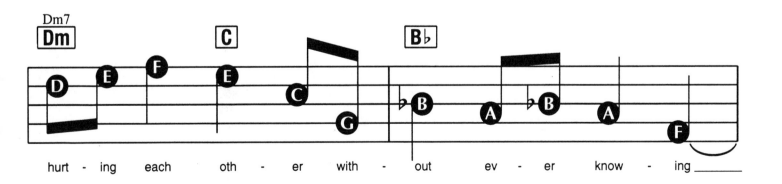

hurt - ing each oth - er with - out ev - er know - ing _____

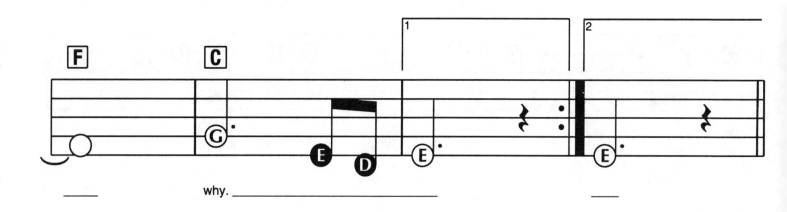

why.

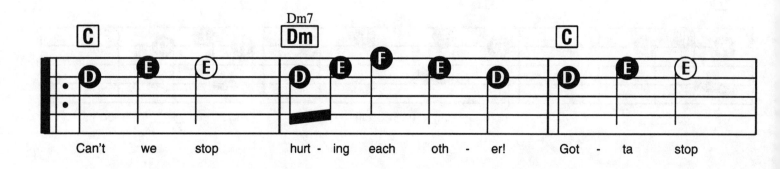

Can't we stop hurt - ing each oth - er! Got - ta stop

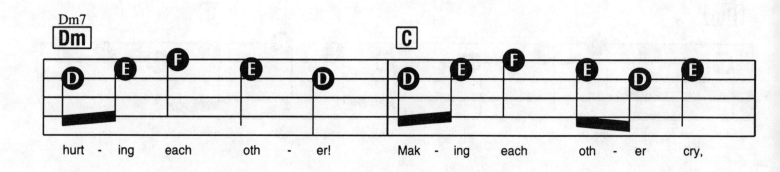

hurt - ing each oth - er! Mak - ing each oth - er cry,

Repeat and Fade

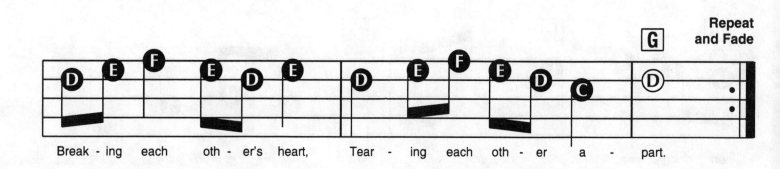

Break - ing each oth - er's heart, Tear - ing each oth - er a - part.

It's Going to Take Some Time

Registration 3
Rhythm: Rock or 8 Beat

Words and Music by Carole King
and Toni Stern

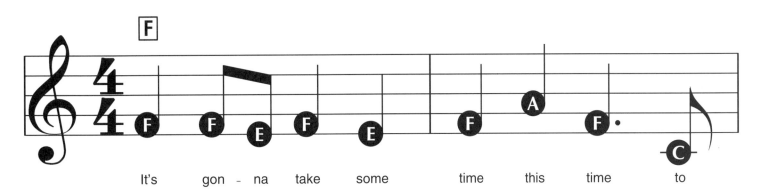

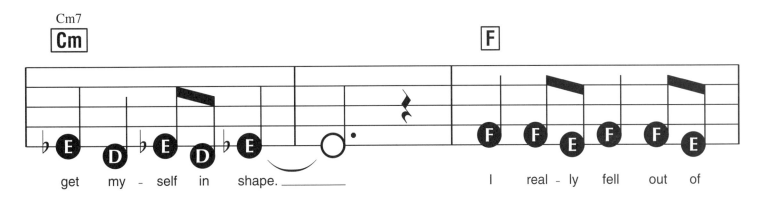

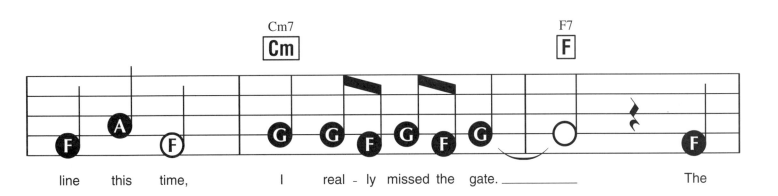

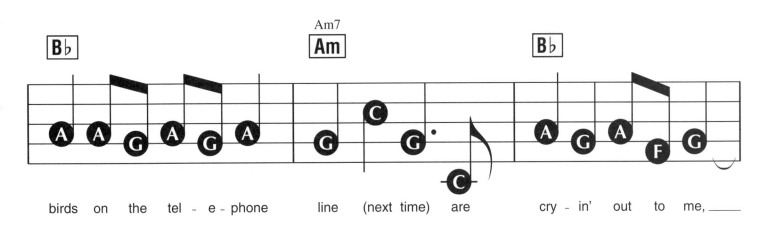

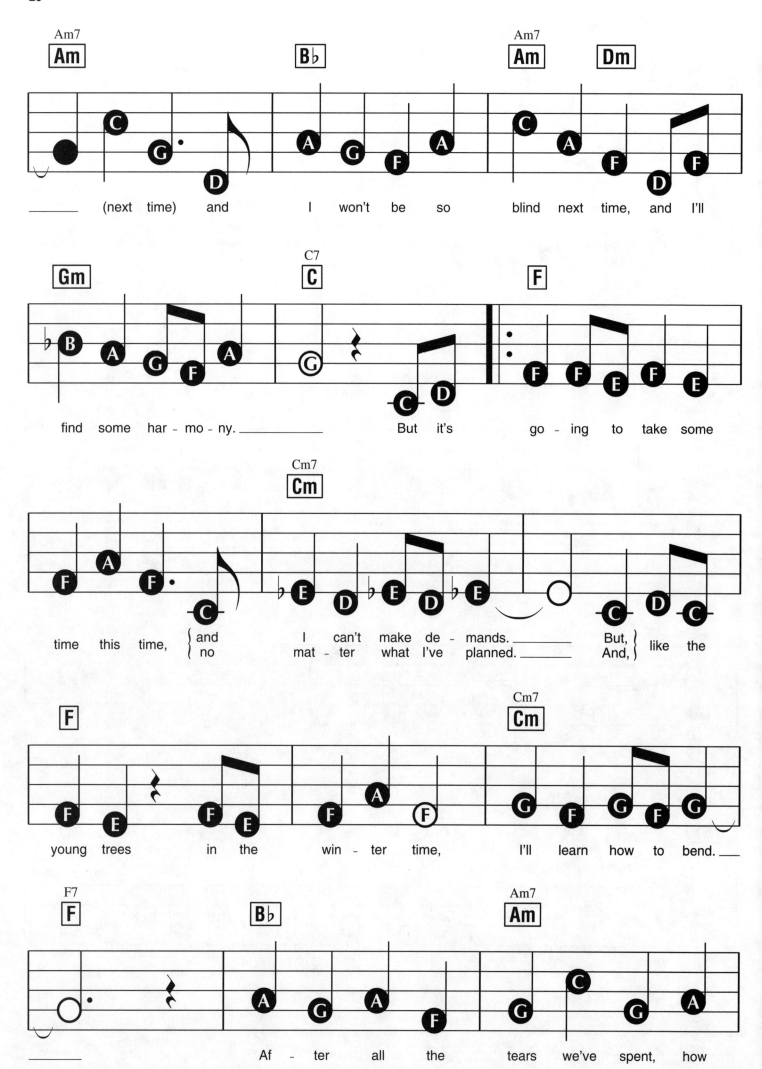

21

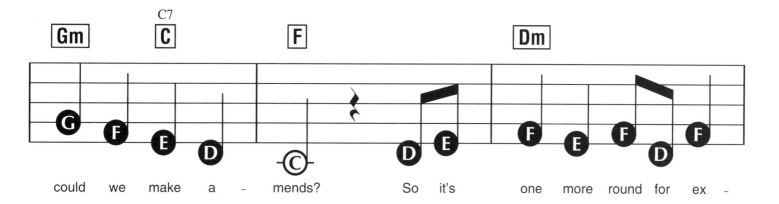

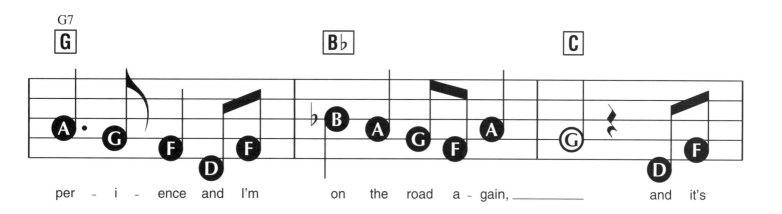

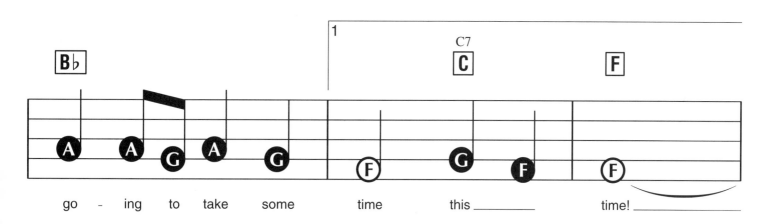

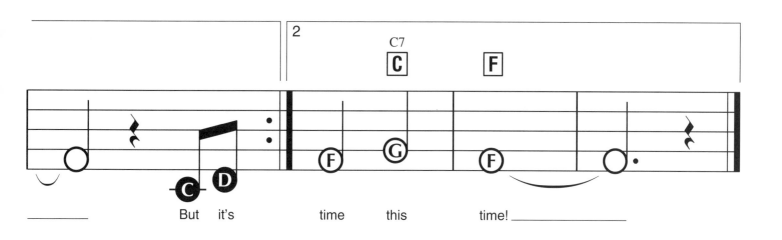

I Won't Last a Day Without You

Registration 8
Rhythm: 4/4 Ballad or 8 Beat

Words and Music by Paul Williams
and Roger Nichols

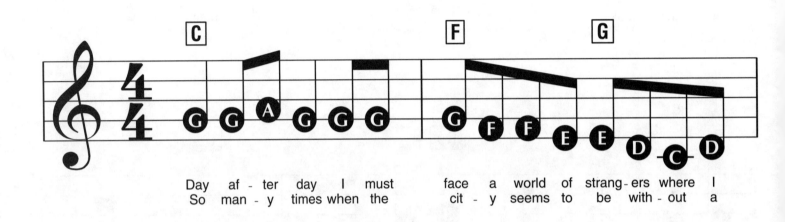

Day af - ter day I must face a world of strang - ers where I
So man - y times when the cit - y seems to be with - out a

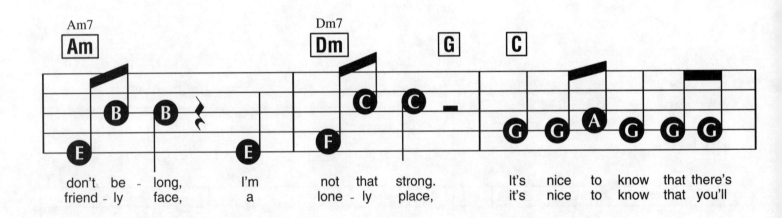

don't be - long, I'm not that strong. It's nice to know that there's
friend - ly face, a lone - ly place, it's nice to know that you'll

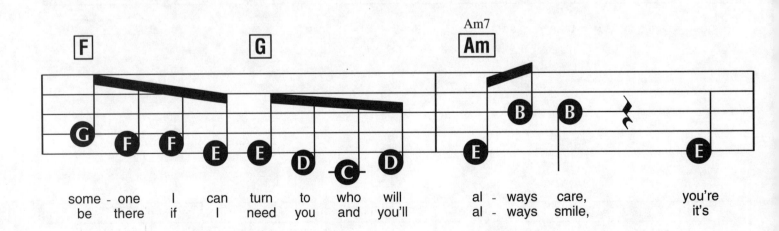

some - one I can turn to who will al - ways care, you're
be there if I need you and you'll al - ways smile, it's

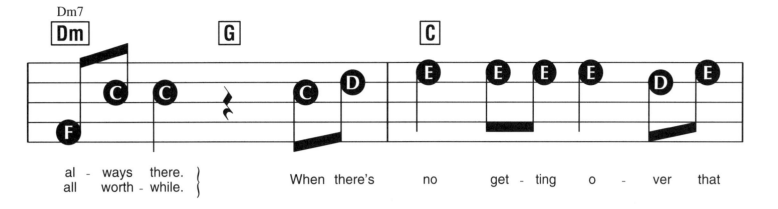

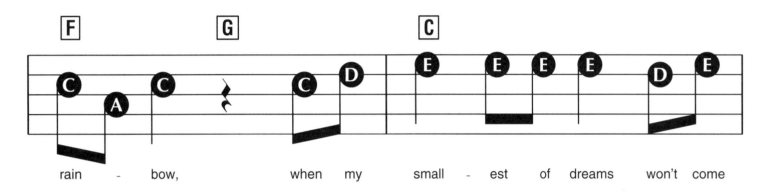

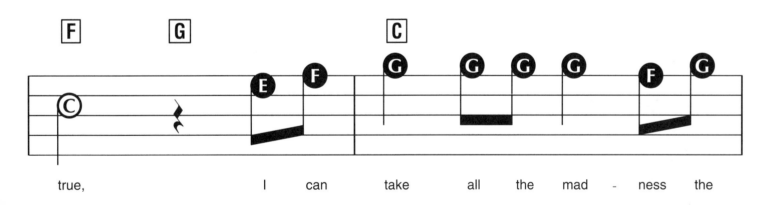

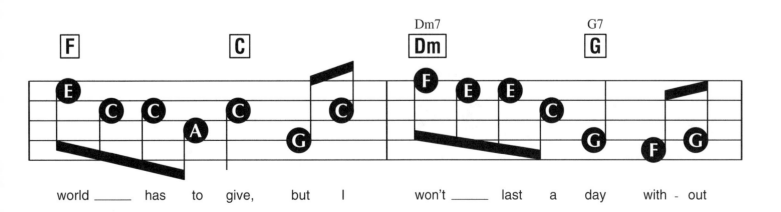

24

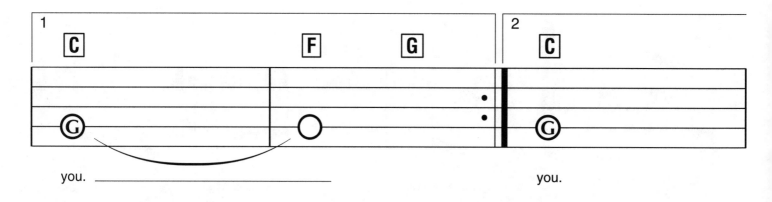

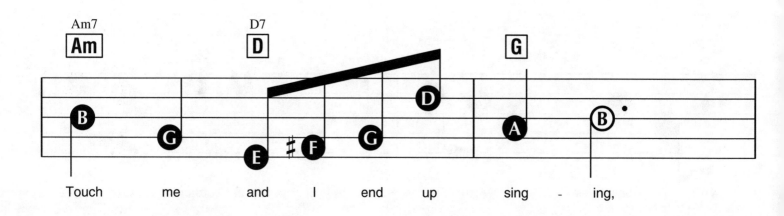

Touch me and I end up sing - ing,

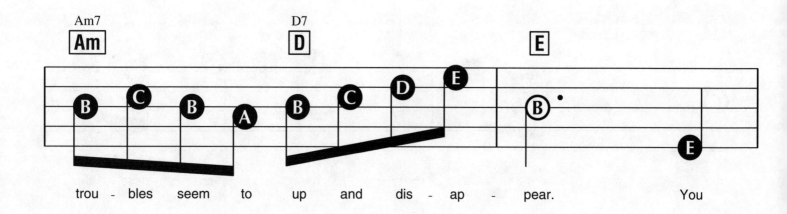

trou - bles seem to up and dis - ap - pear. You

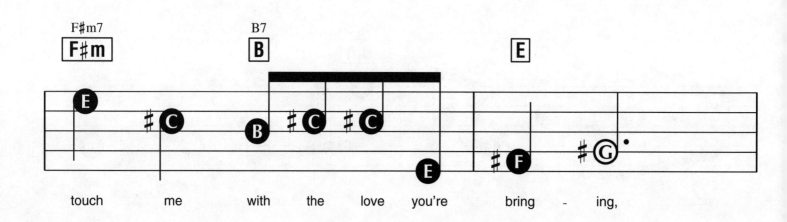

touch me with the love you're bring - ing,

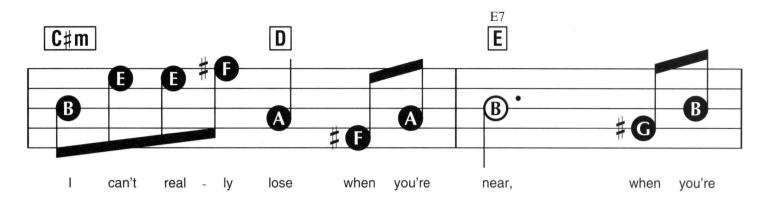

I can't real - ly lose when you're near, when you're

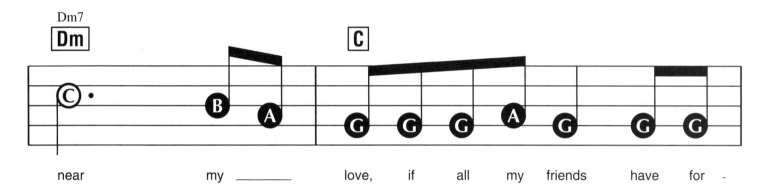

near my _____ love, if all my friends have for -

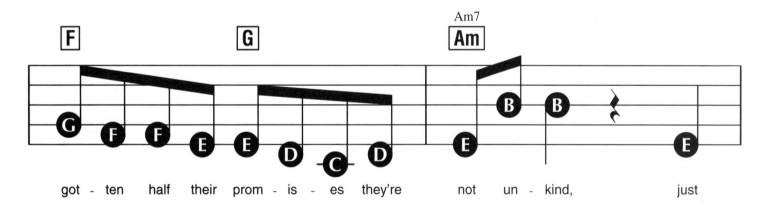

got - ten half their prom - is - es they're not un - kind, just

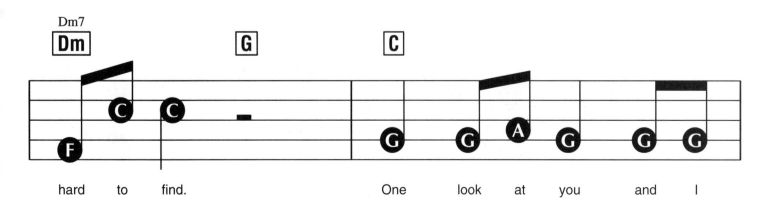

hard to find. One look at you and I

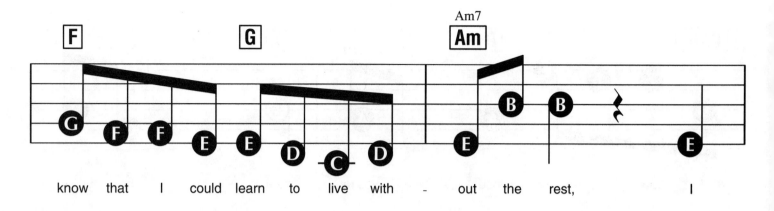

know that I could learn to live with - out the rest, I

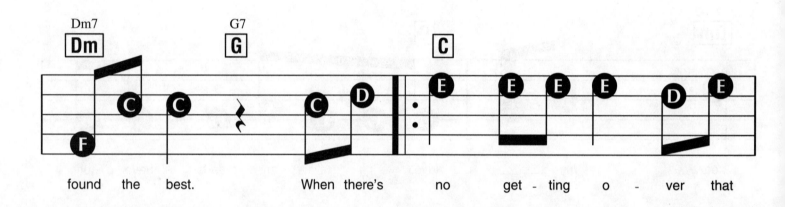

found the best. When there's no get - ting o - ver that

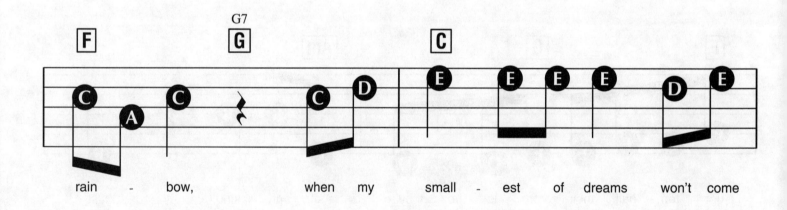

rain - bow, when my small - est of dreams won't come

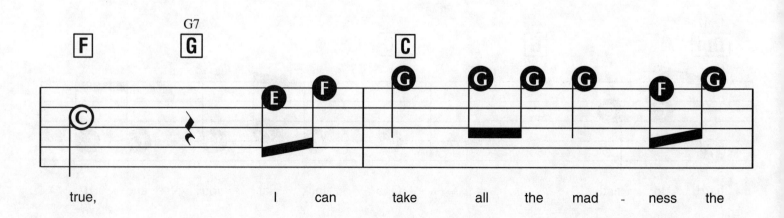

true, I can take all the mad - ness the

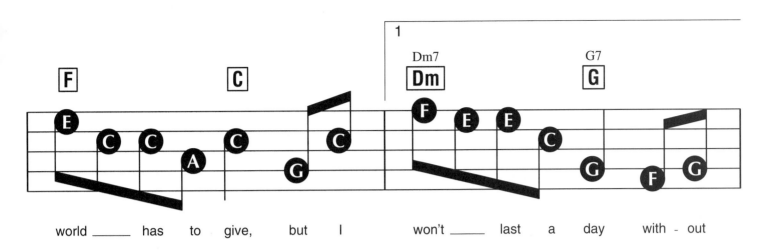

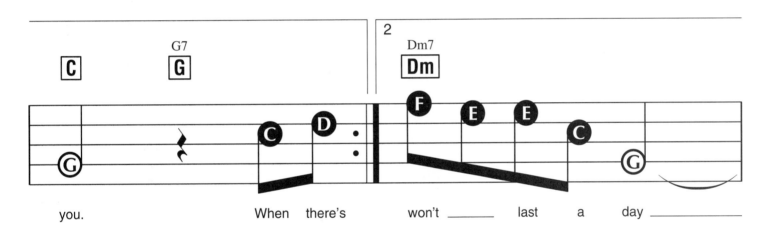

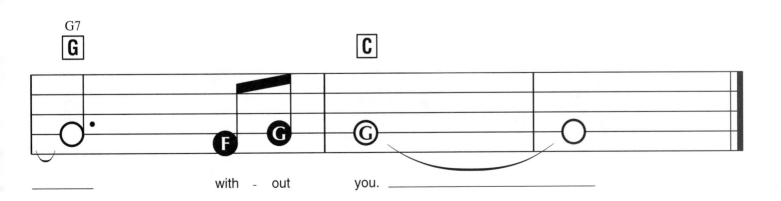

Merry Christmas, Darling

Registration 9
Rhythm: 4/4 Ballad

Words and Music by Richard Carpenter
and Frank Pooler

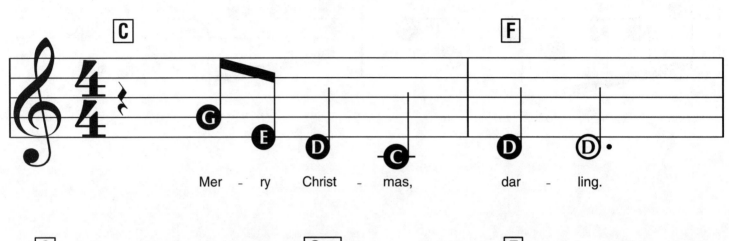

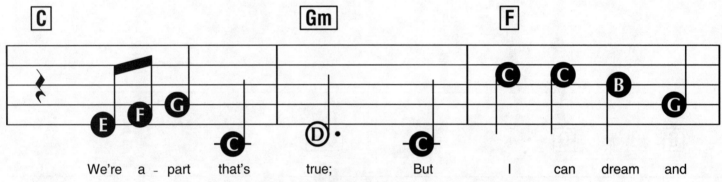

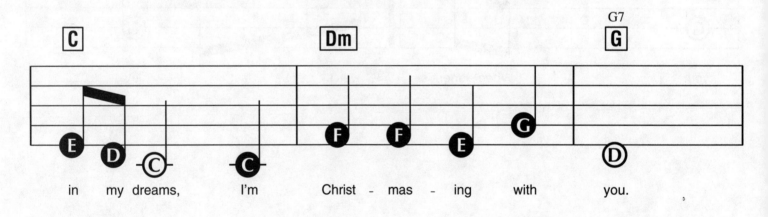

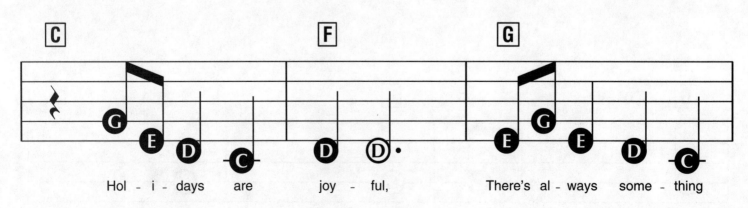

29

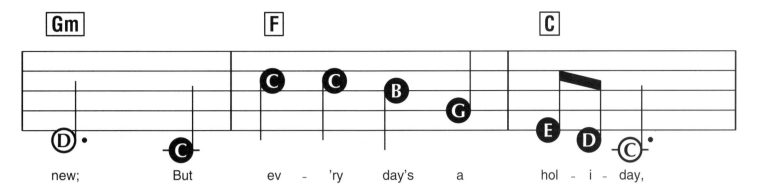

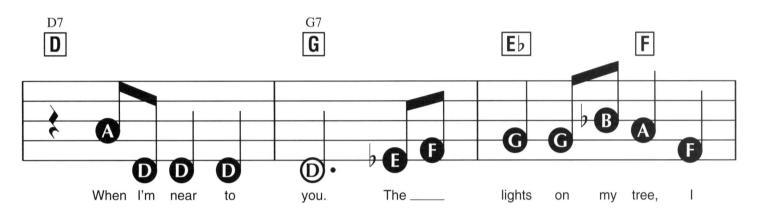

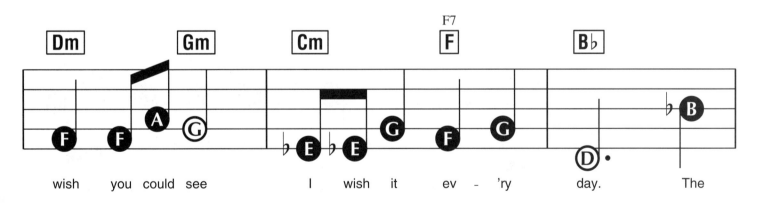

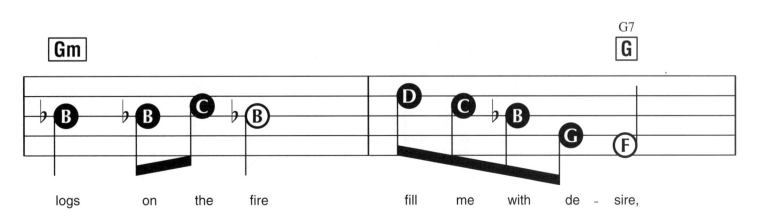

30

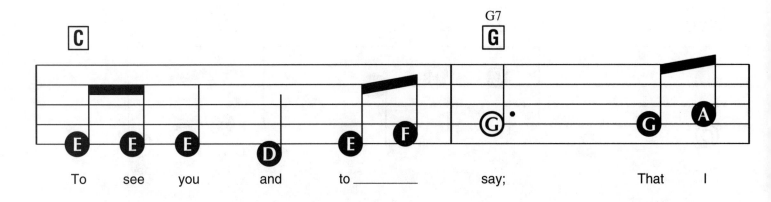

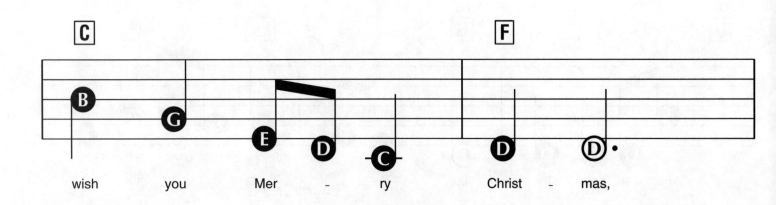

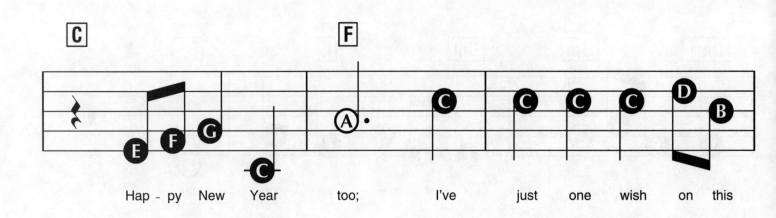

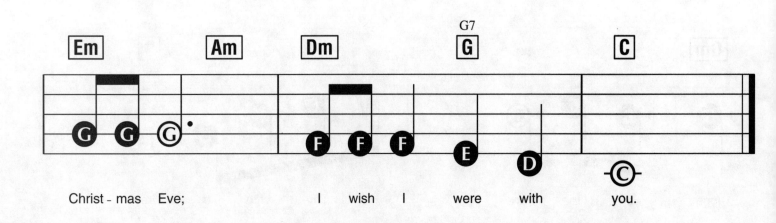

Only Yesterday

Registration 8
Rhythm: 4/4 Ballad or Rock

Words and Music by Richard Carpenter
and John Bettis

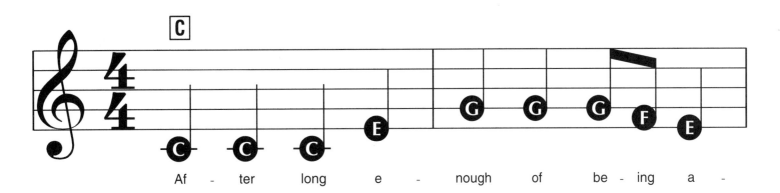

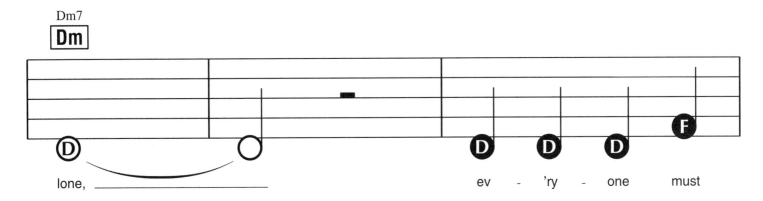

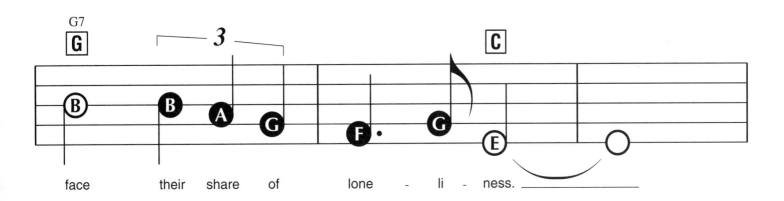

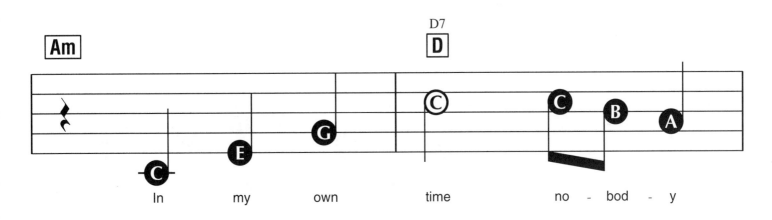

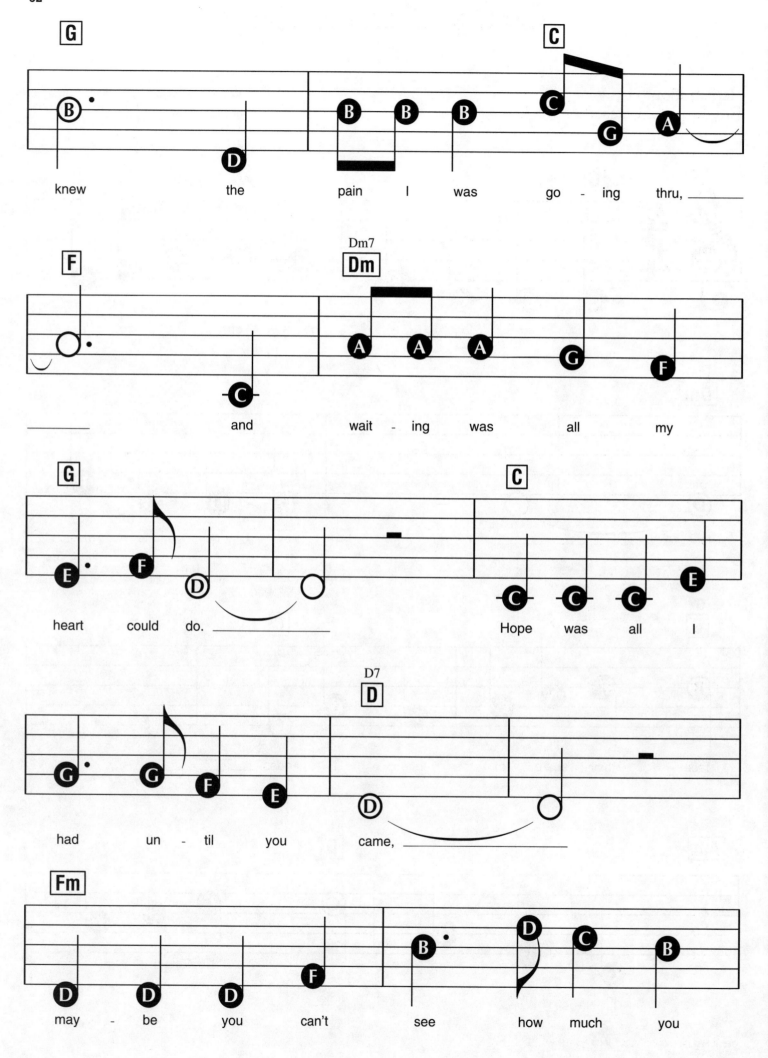

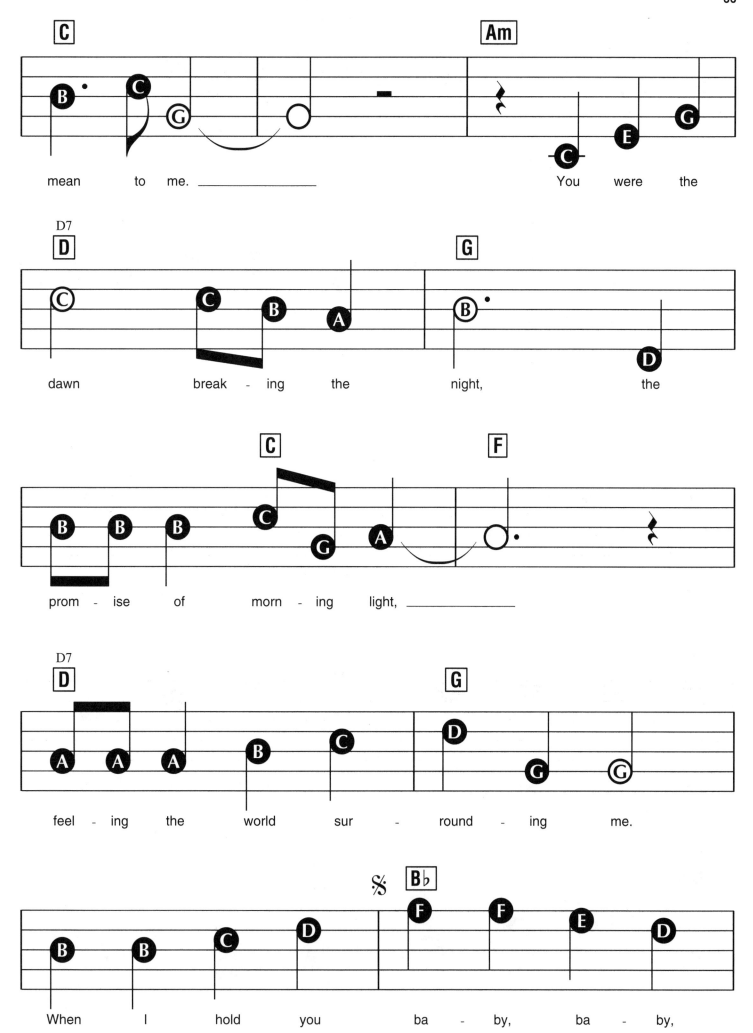

34

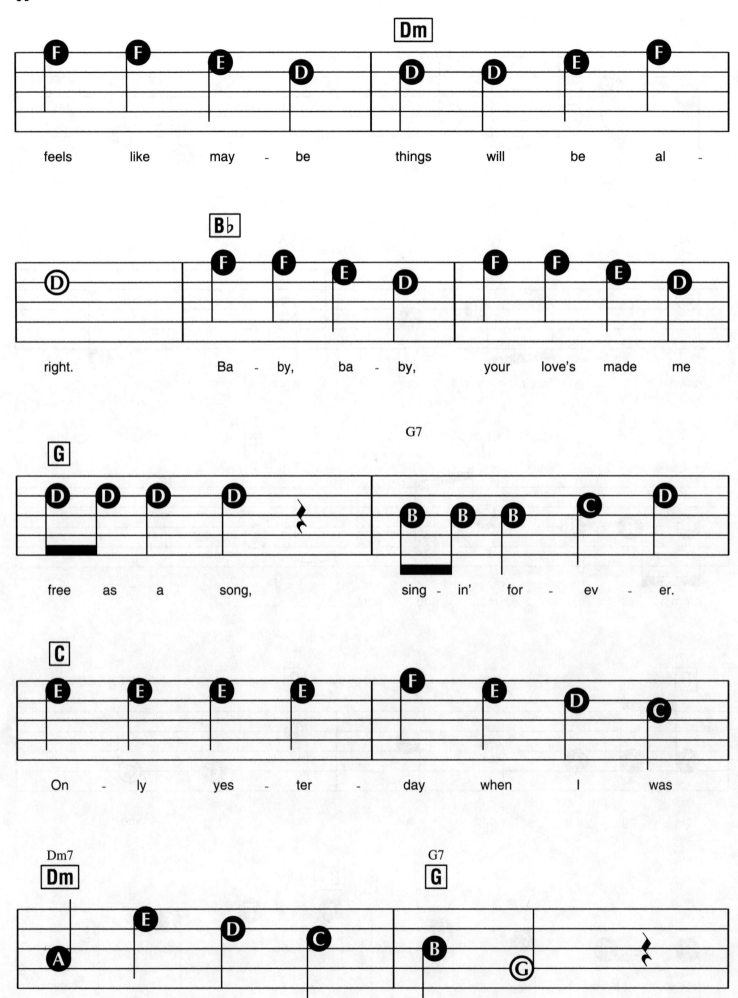

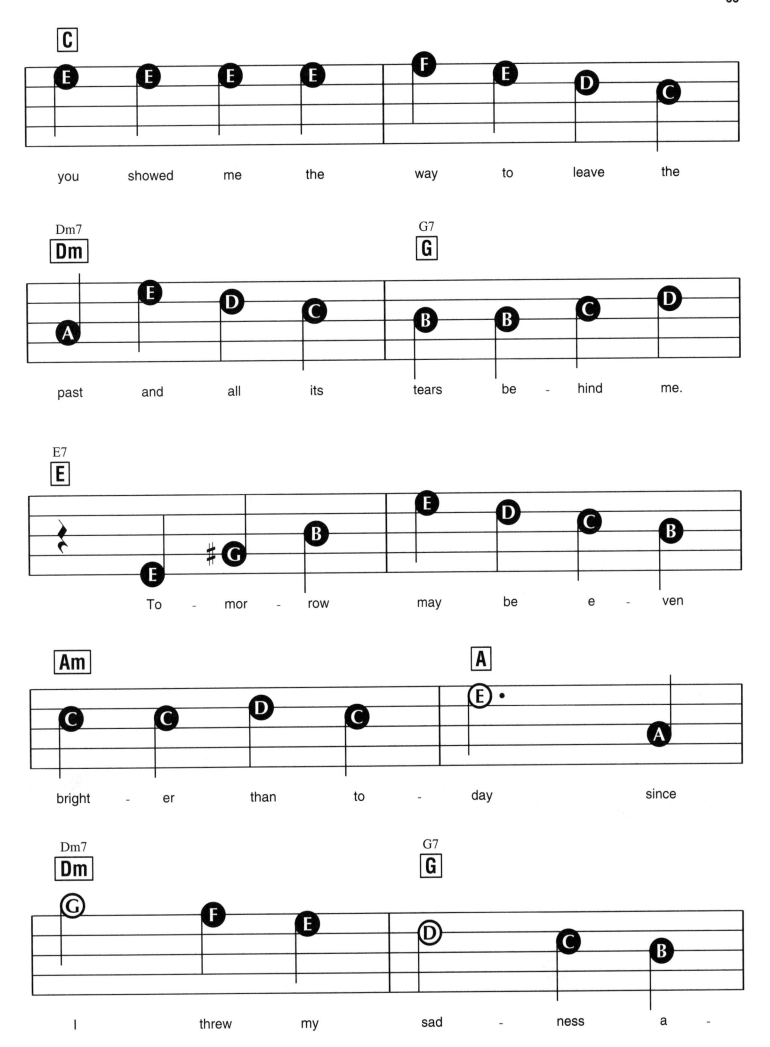

36

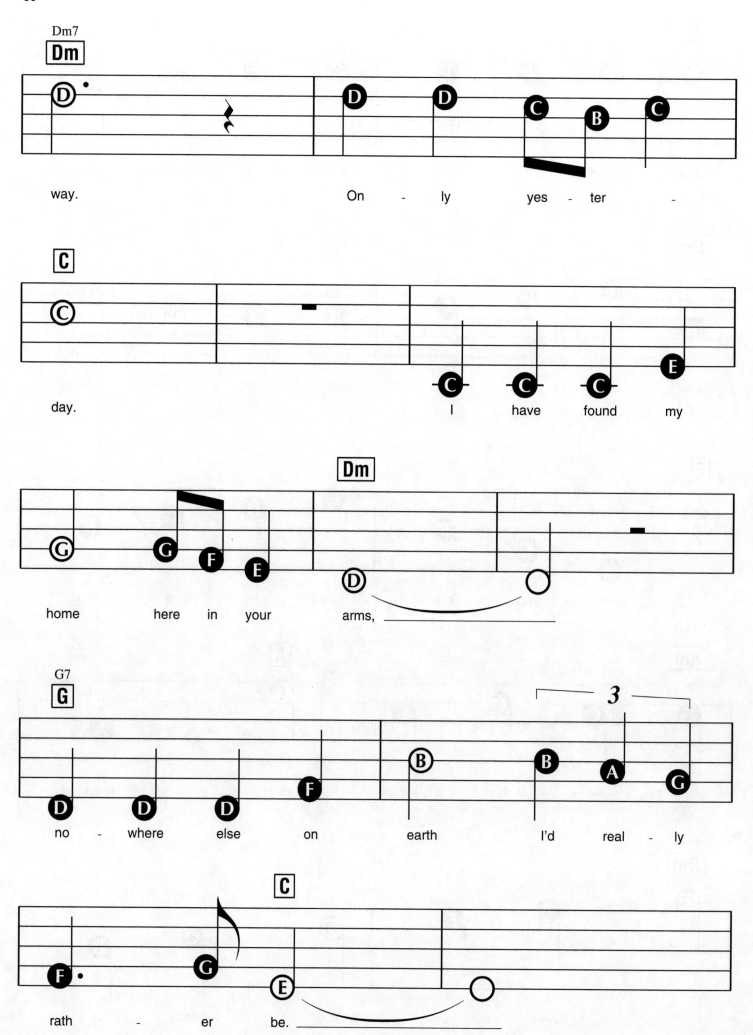

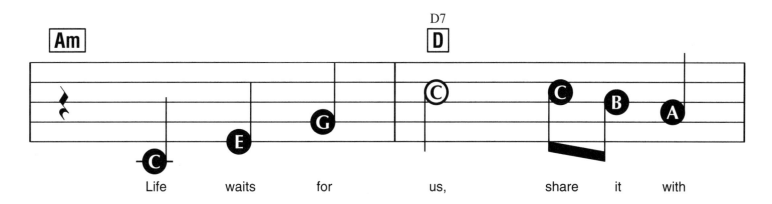

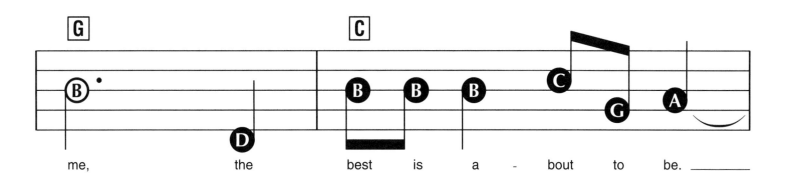

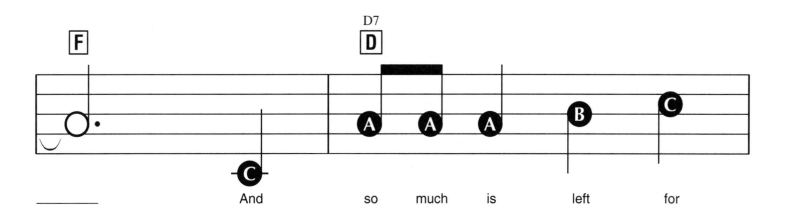

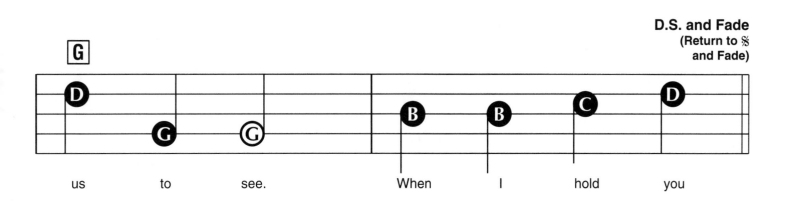

Please Mr. Postman

Registration 1
Rhythm: Slow Rock or 12 Beat

Words and Music by Robert Bateman, Georgia Dobbins,
William Garrett, Freddie Gorman and Brian Holland

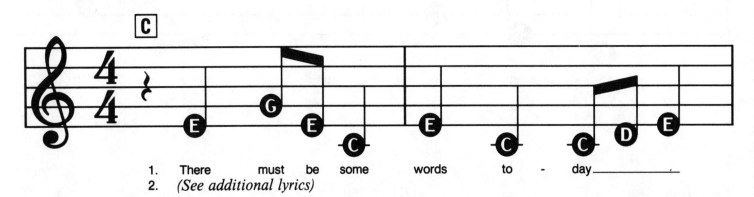

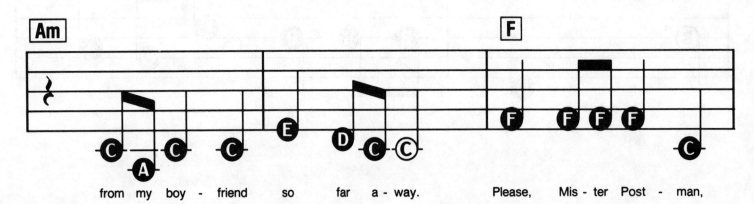

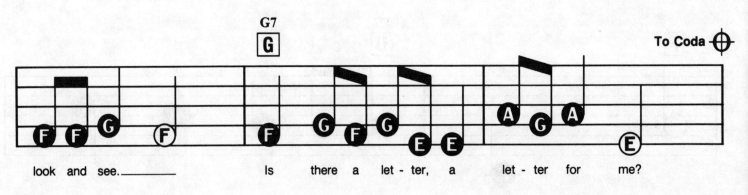

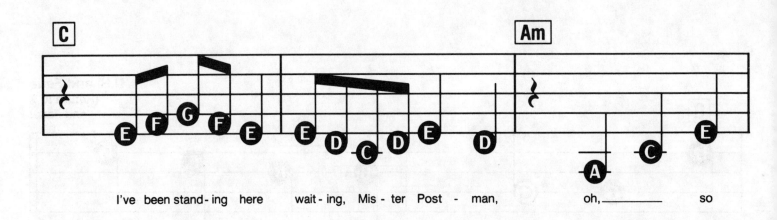

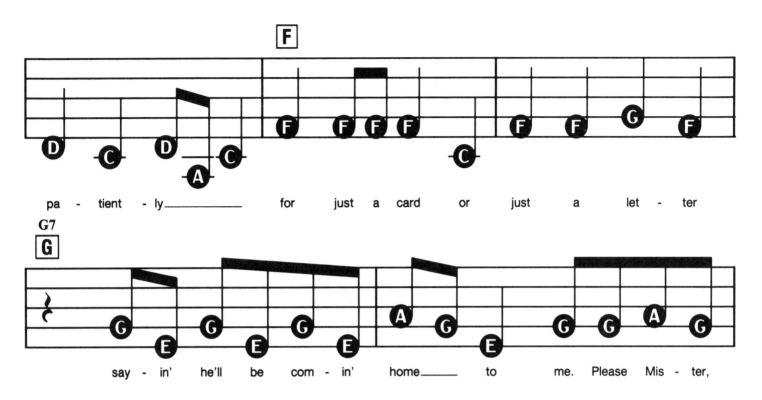

pa - tient - ly_____ for just a card or just a let - ter

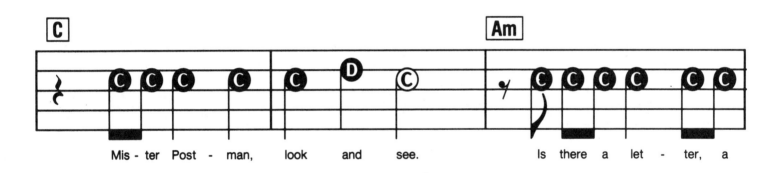

say - in' he'll be com - in' home____ to me. Please Mis - ter,

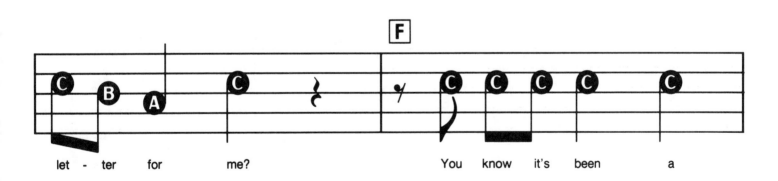

Mis - ter Post - man, look and see. Is there a let - ter, a

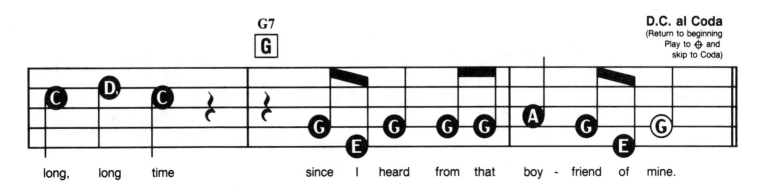

let - ter for me? You know it's been a

D.C. al Coda
(Return to beginning
Play to ⊕ and
skip to Coda)

long, long time since I heard from that boy - friend of mine.

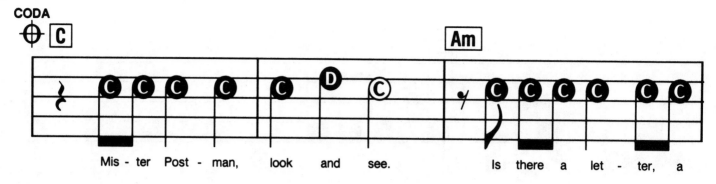

Mis - ter Post - man, look and see. Is there a let - ter, a

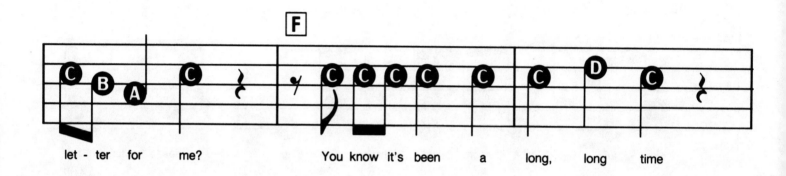

let - ter for me? You know it's been a long, long time

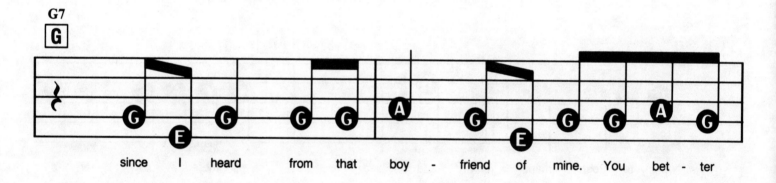

since I heard from that boy - friend of mine. You bet - ter

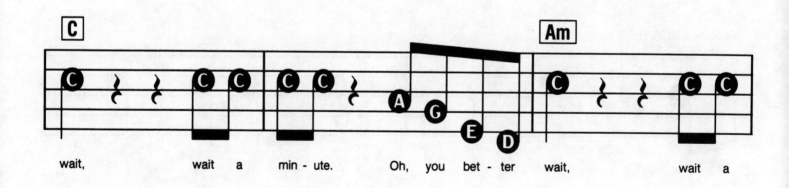

wait, wait a min - ute. Oh, you bet - ter wait, wait a

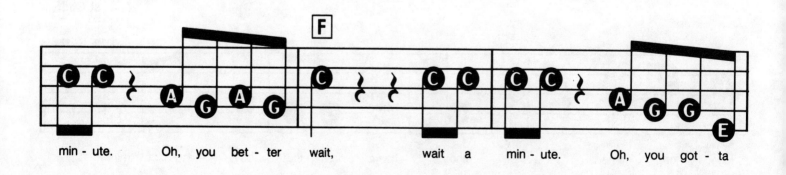

min - ute. Oh, you bet - ter wait, wait a min - ute. Oh, you got - ta

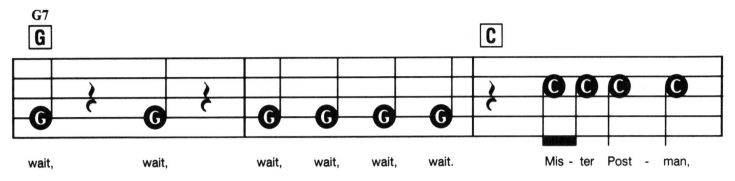

wait, wait, wait, wait, wait, wait. Mis - ter Post - man,

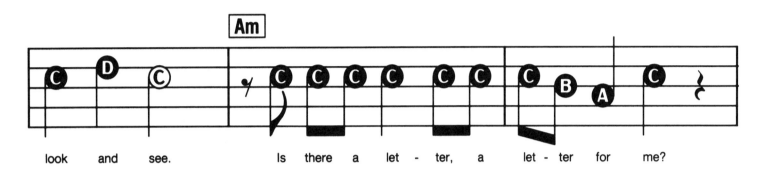

look and see. Is there a let - ter, a let - ter for me?

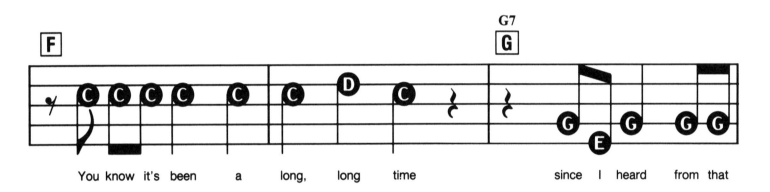

You know it's been a long, long time since I heard from that

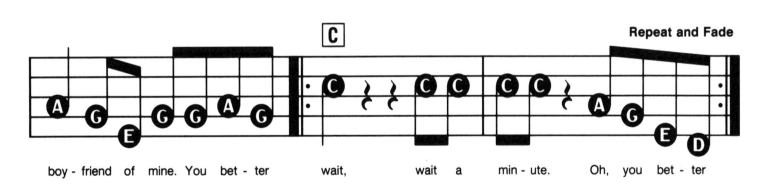

boy - friend of mine. You bet - ter wait, wait a min - ute. Oh, you bet - ter

ADDITIONAL LYRICS

2. So many days have passed me by.
   You saw the tears in my eyes.
   You wouldn't stop to make me feel better
   By leavin' me a card or a letter.

Rainy Days and Mondays

Registration 1
Rhythm: Rock or Pops

Lyrics by Paul Williams
Music by Roger Nichols

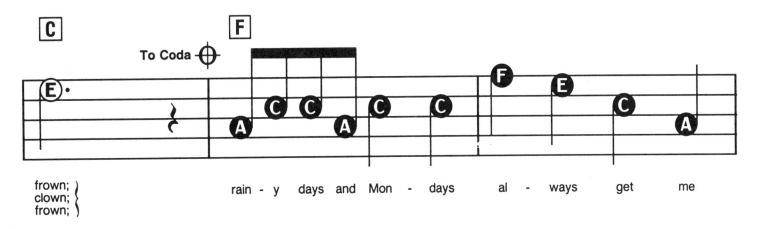

frown;
clown;
frown;

rain - y days and Mon - days al - ways get me

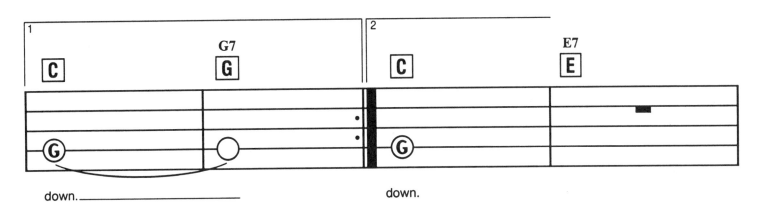

down. _____ down.

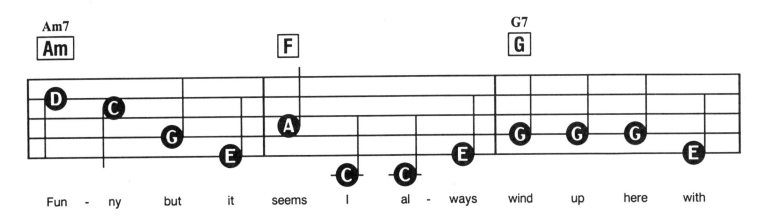

Fun - ny but it seems I al - ways wind up here with

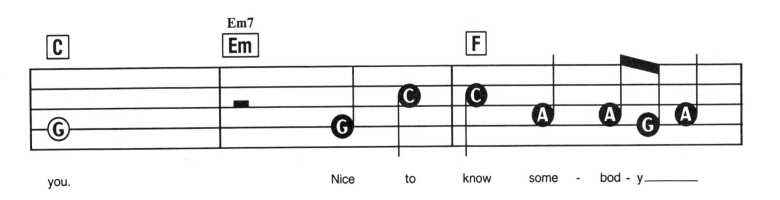

you. Nice to know some - bod - y _____

44

Superstar

Registration 8
Rhythm: 8 Beat or Rock

Words and Music by Leon Russell
and Bonnie Sheridan

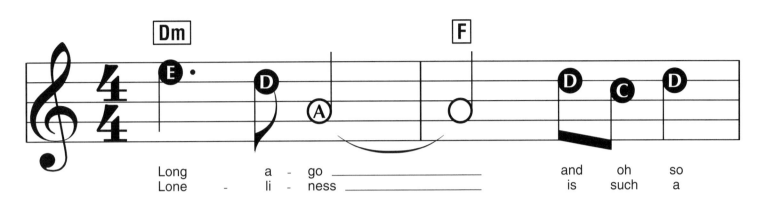

Long a - go _____ and oh so a
Lone - li - ness _____ is such a

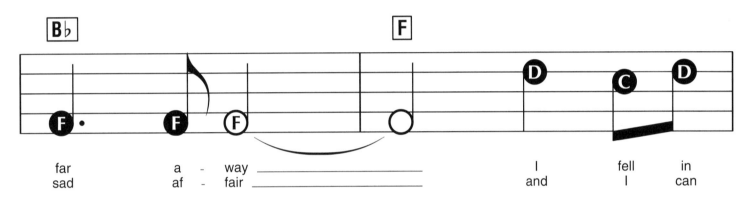

far a - way _____ I fell in
sad af - fair _____ and I can

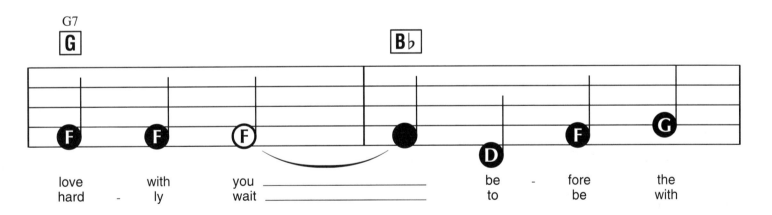

love with you _____ be - fore the
hard - ly wait _____ to be with

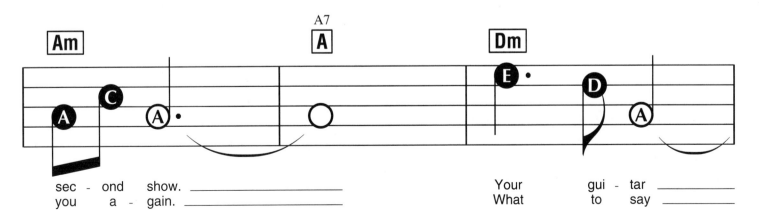

sec - ond show. _____
you a - gain. _____

Your gui - tar _____
What to say _____

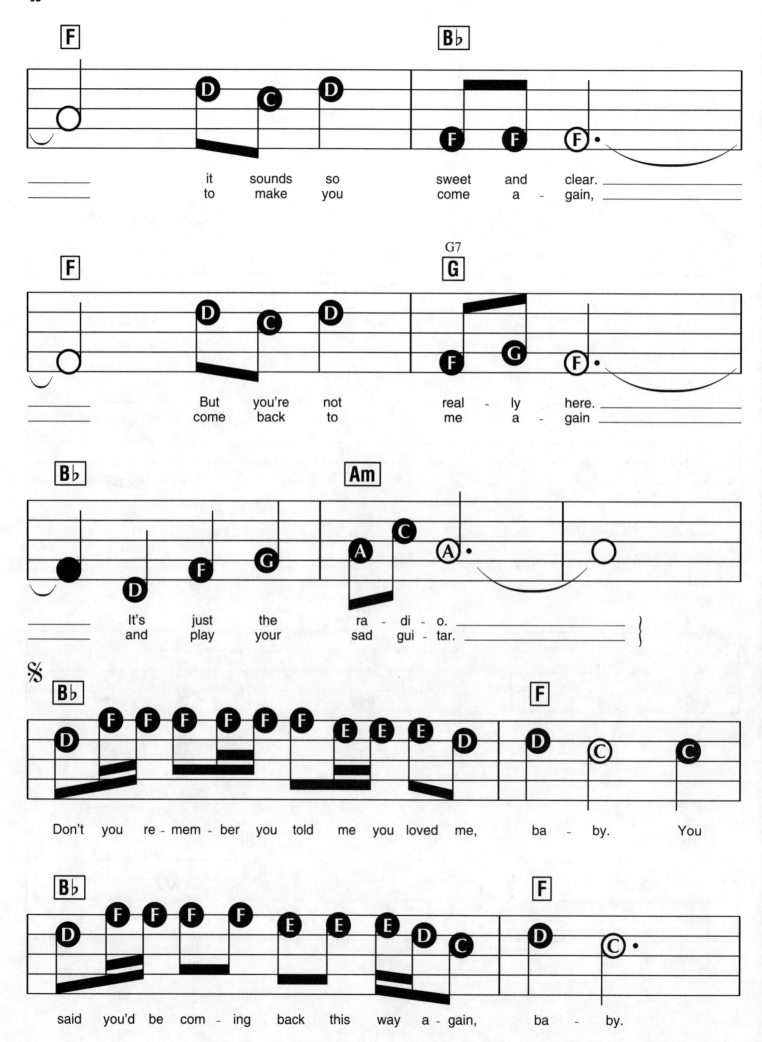

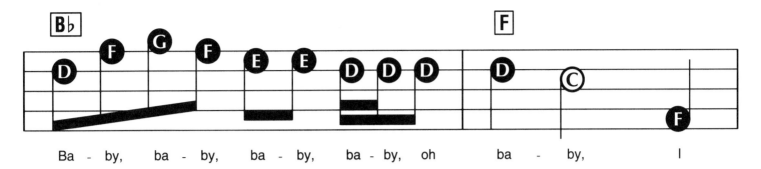

Ba - by, ba - by, ba - by, ba - by, oh ba - by, I

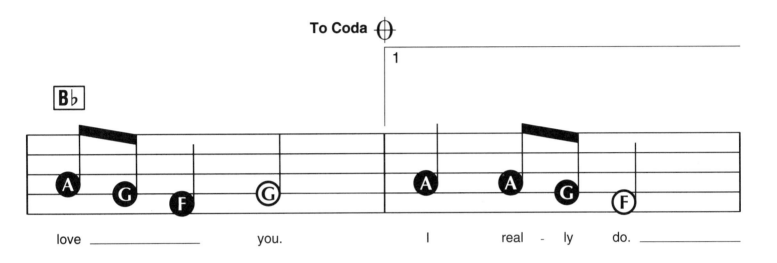

love _____ you. I real - ly do. _____

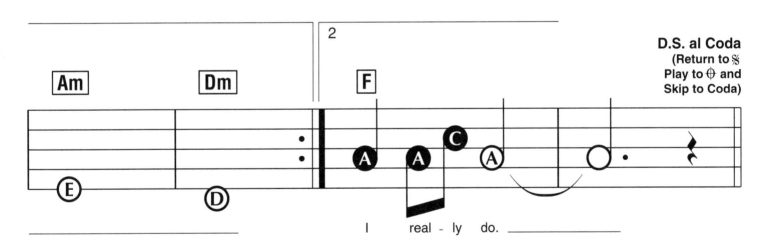

I real - ly do. _____

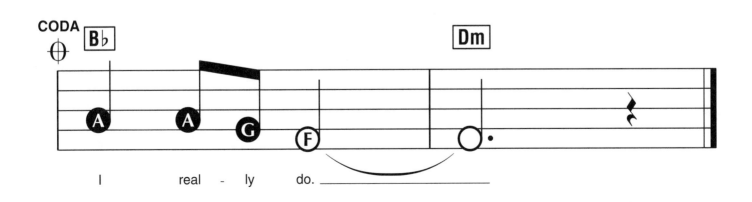

I real - ly do. _____

Sing

Registration 8
Rhythm: Rock or 8 Beat

Words and Music by
Joe Raposo

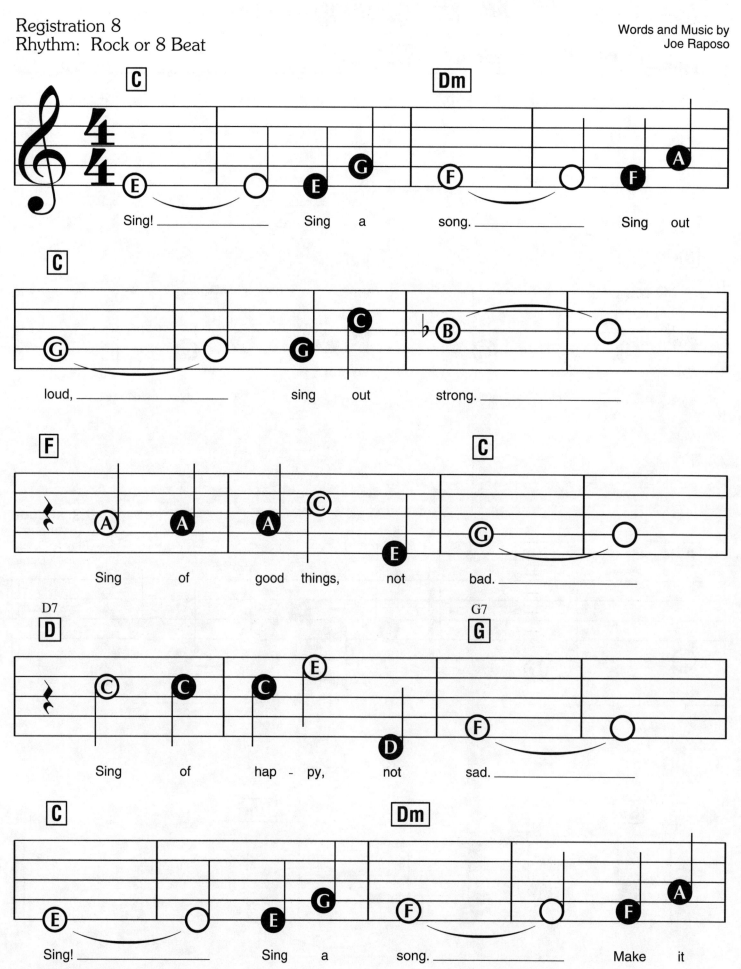

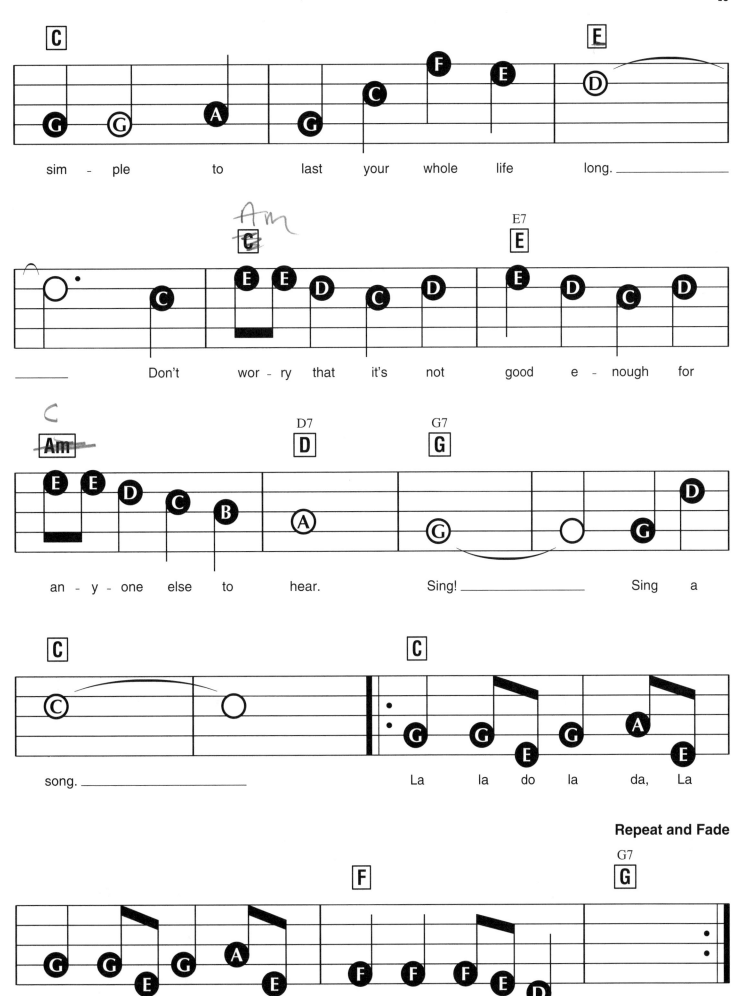

Top of the World

Registration 2
Rhythm: Fox Trot

Words and Music by John Bettis
and Richard Carpenter

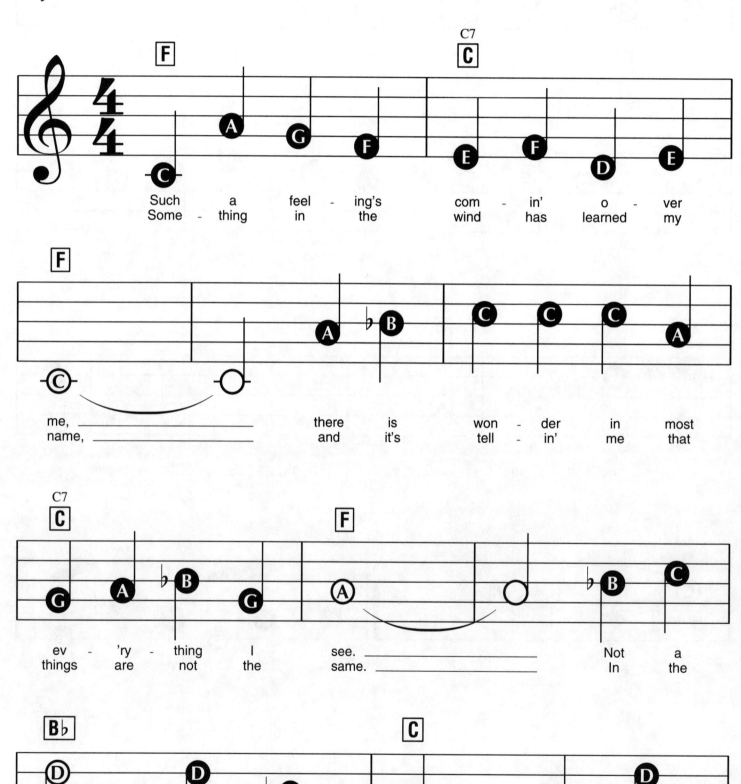

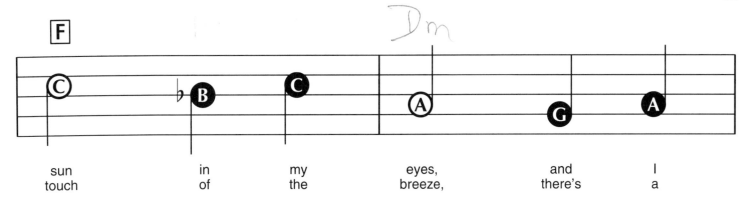

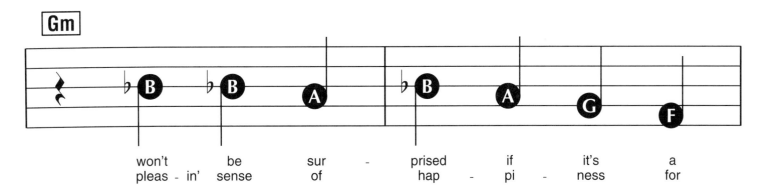

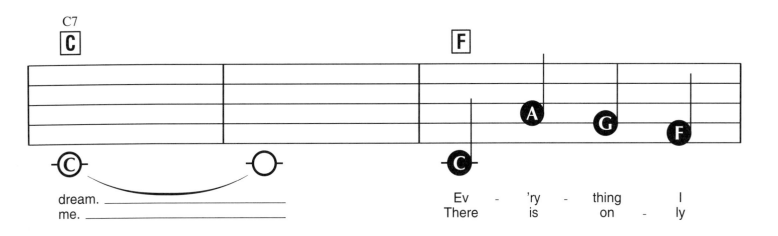

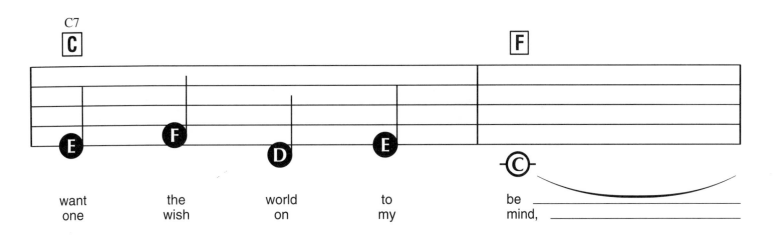

52

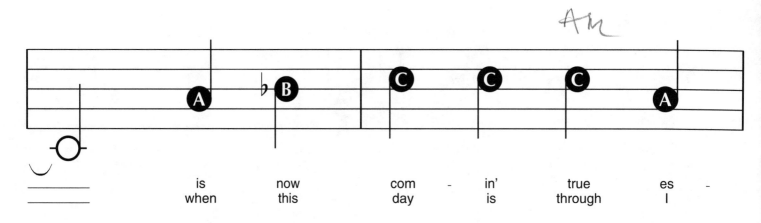

is   now   com - in'   true   es -
when   this   day   is   through   I

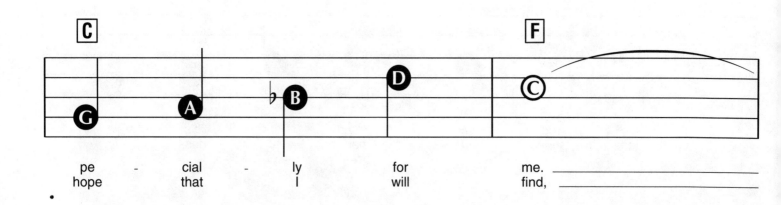

pe   -   cial -   ly   for   me. _____
hope   that   I   will   find, _____

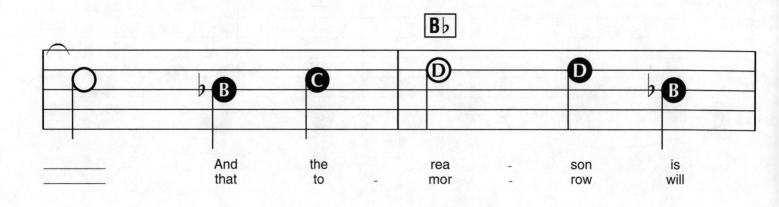

_____   And   the   rea - son   is
              that   to -   mor - row   will

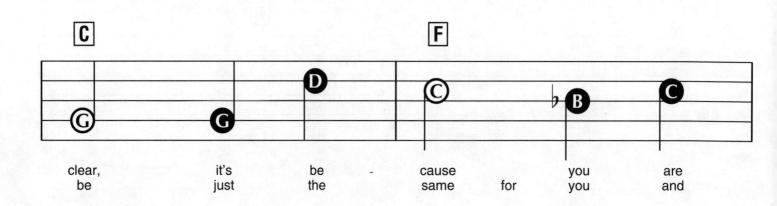

clear,   it's   be - cause   you   are
be   just   the   same   for   you   and

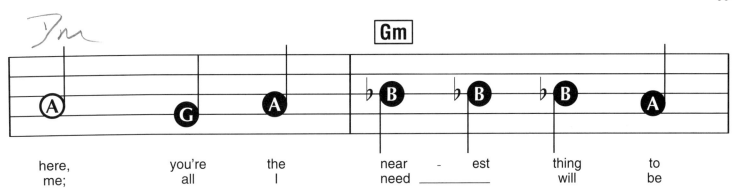

here,   you're   the   near - est   thing   to
me;   all   I   need _____   will   be

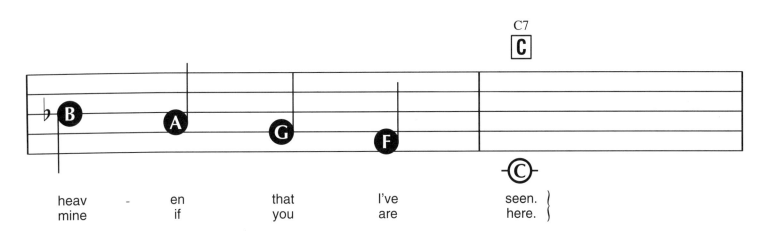

heav - en   that   I've   seen.
mine   if   you   are   here.

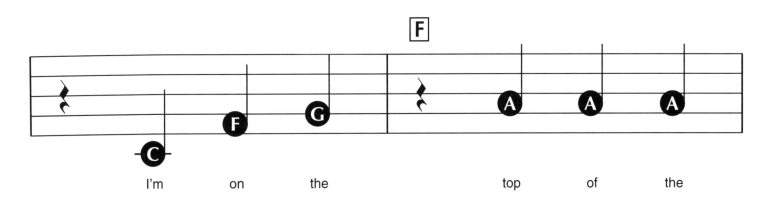

I'm   on   the   top   of   the

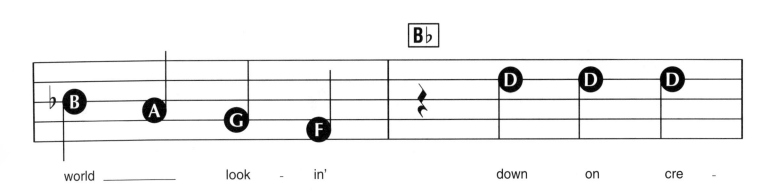

world _____   look - in'   down   on   cre -

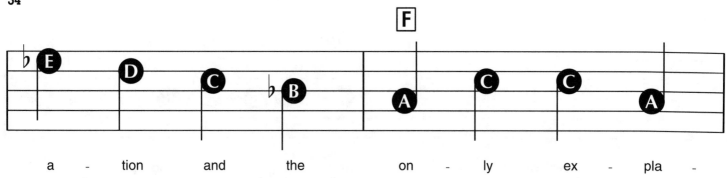

a - tion and the on - ly ex - pla -

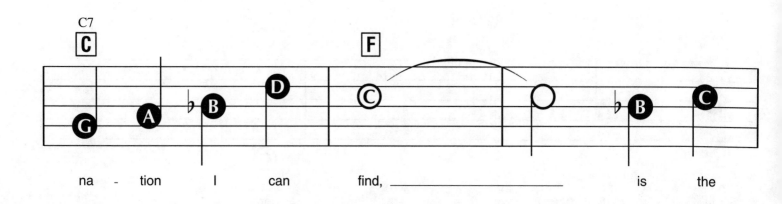

na - tion I can find, _____ is the

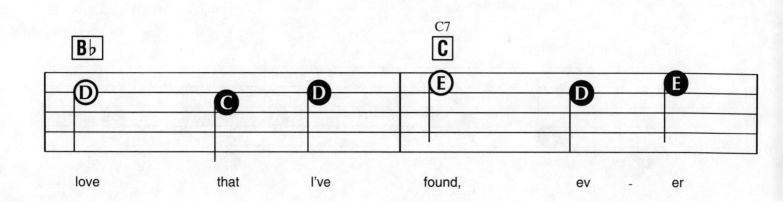

love that I've found, ev - er

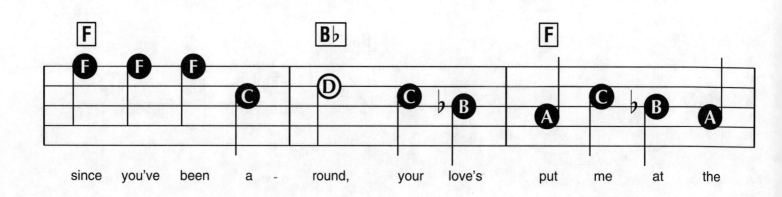

since you've been a - round, your love's put me at the

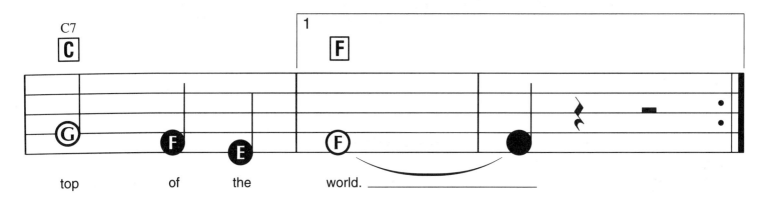

top   of   the   world. _____

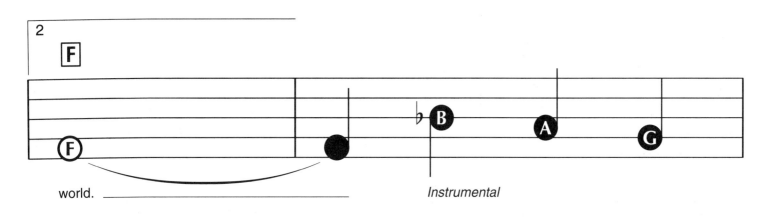

world. _____   *Instrumental*

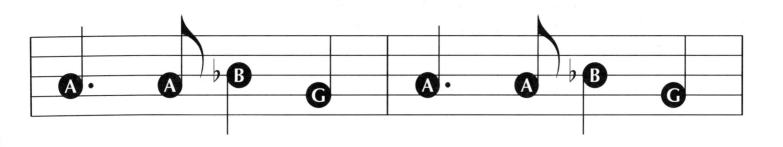

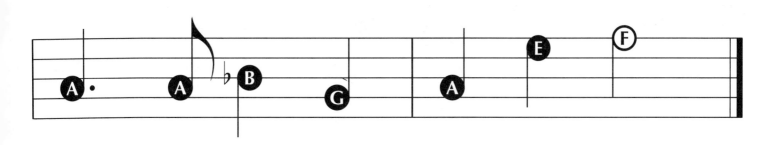

We've Only Just Begun

Registration 9
Rhythm: 8 Beat or Pops

Words and Music by Roger Nichols
and Paul Williams

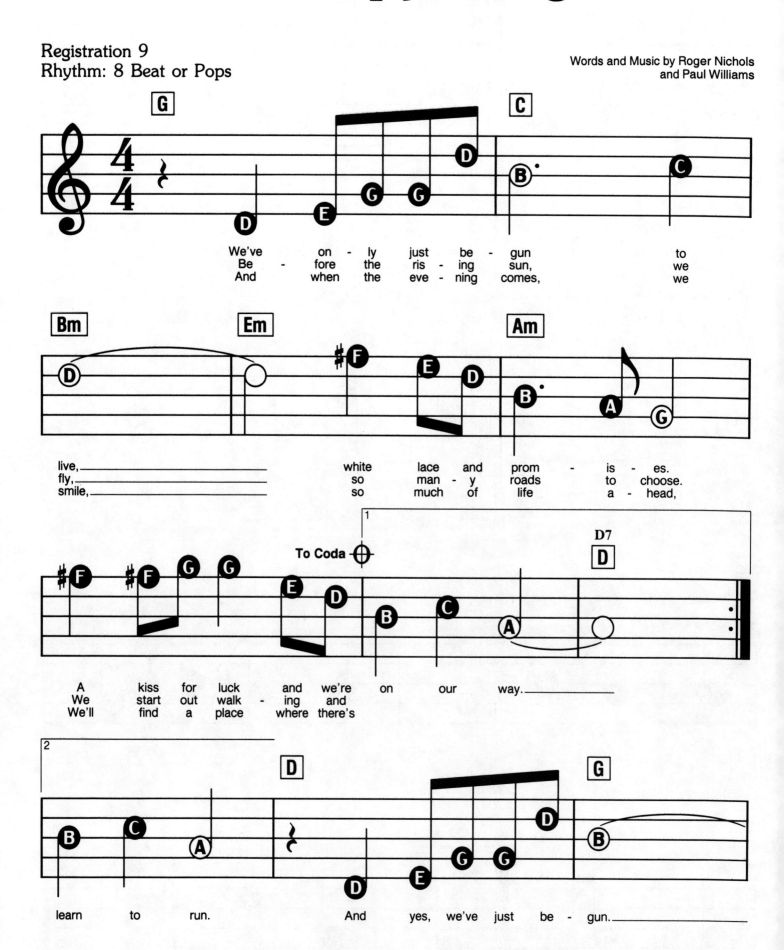

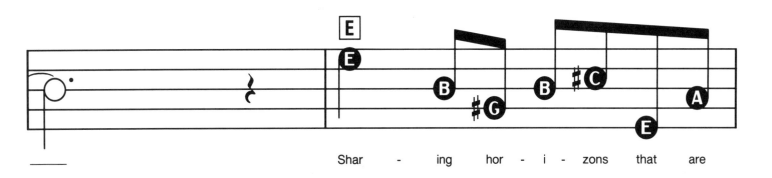

Shar - ing hor - i - zons that are

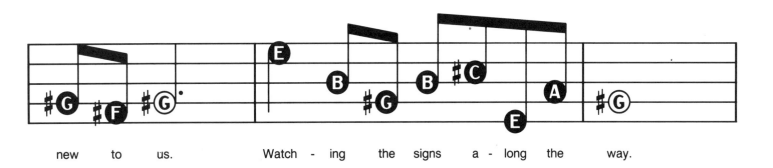

new to us. Watch - ing the signs a - long the way.

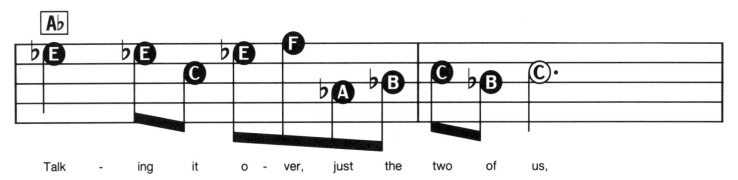

Talk - ing it o - ver, just the two of us,

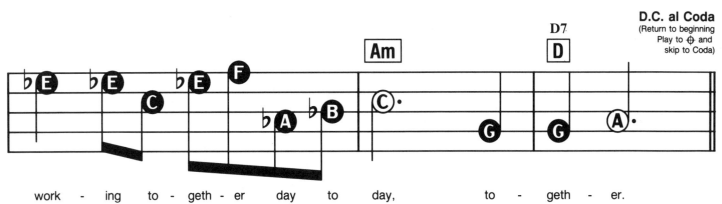

work - ing to - geth - er day to day, to - geth - er.

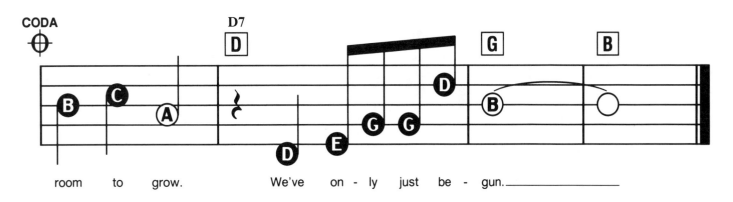

room to grow. We've on - ly just be - gun.

Yesterday Once More

Registration 1
Rhythm: Pop or Rock

Words and Music by John Bettis
and Richard Carpenter

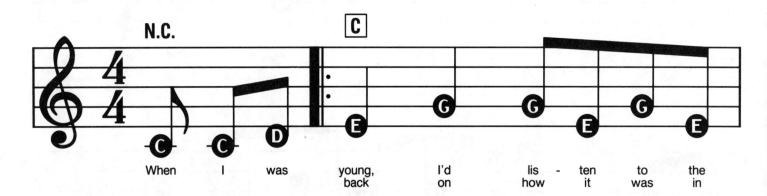

When I was young, I'd lis - ten to the
back on how it was in

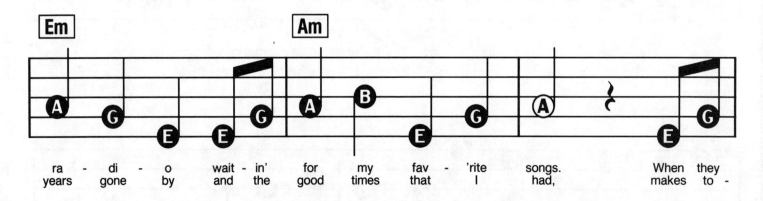

ra - di - o wait - in' for my fav - 'rite songs. When they
years gone by and the good times that I had, makes to -

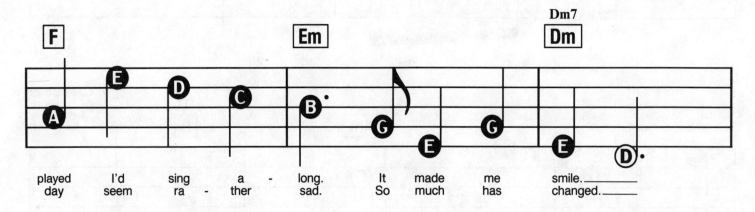

played I'd sing a - long. It made me smile._____
day seem ra - ther sad. So much has changed._____

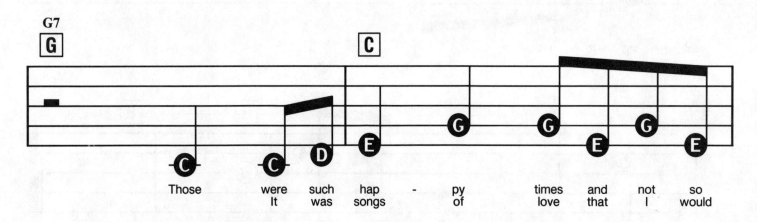

Those were such hap - py times and not so
It was songs of love that I would

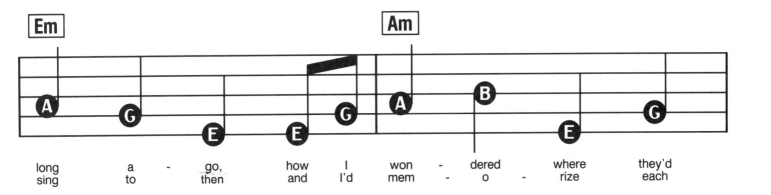
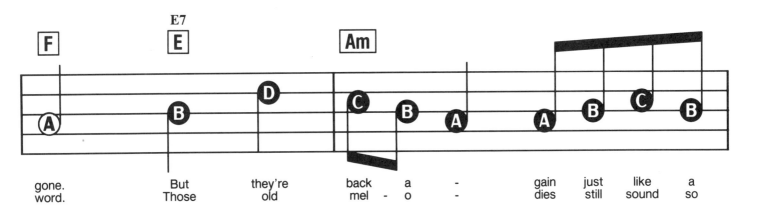
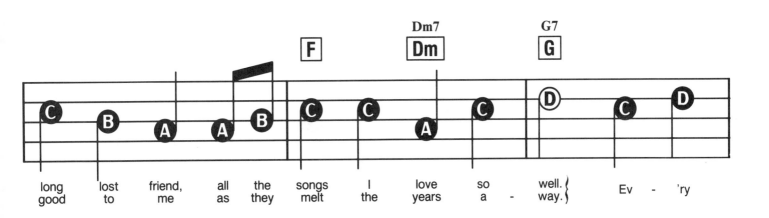
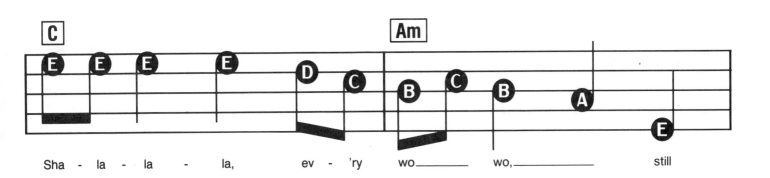

60

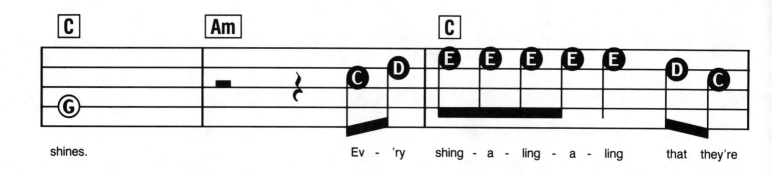

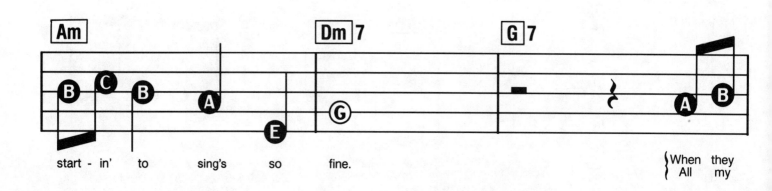

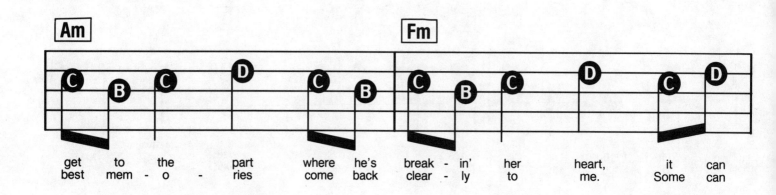

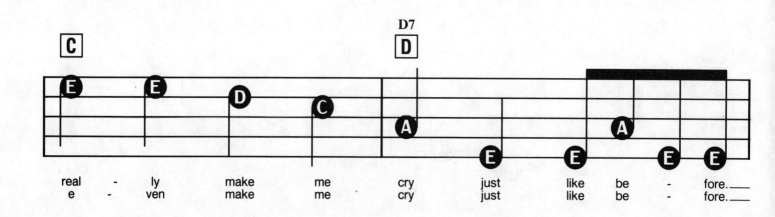

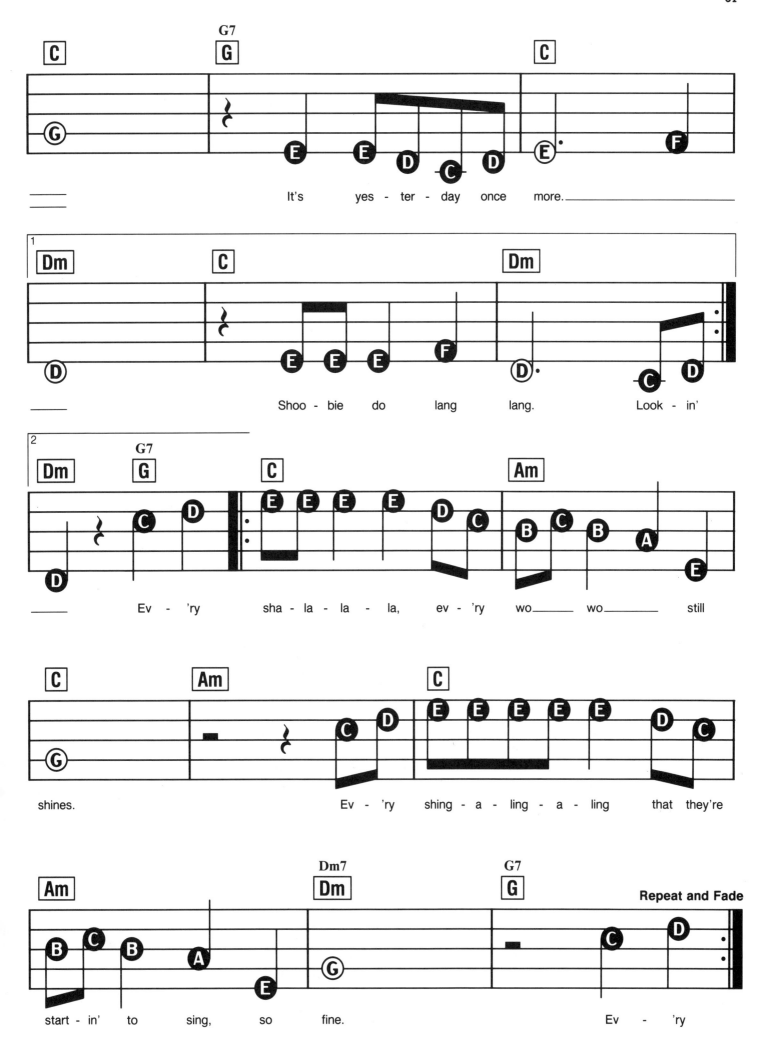

 # Registration Guide

- Match the Registration number on the song to the corresponding numbered category below. Select and activate an instrumental sound available on your instrument.

- Choose an automatic rhythm appropriate to the mood and style of the song. (Consult your Owner's Guide for proper operation of automatic rhythm features.)

- Adjust the tempo and volume controls to comfortable settings.

Registration

1	Mellow	Flutes, Clarinet, Oboe, Flugel Horn, Trombone, French Horn, Organ Flutes
2	Ensemble	Brass Section, Sax Section, Wind Ensemble, Full Organ, Theater Organ
3	Strings	Violin, Viola, Cello, Fiddle, String Ensemble, Pizzicato, Organ Strings
4	Guitars	Acoustic/Electric Guitars, Banjo, Mandolin, Dulcimer, Ukulele, Hawaiian Guitar
5	Mallets	Vibraphone, Marimba, Xylophone, Steel Drums, Bells, Celesta, Chimes
6	Liturgical	Pipe Organ, Hand Bells, Vocal Ensemble, Choir, Organ Flutes
7	Bright	Saxophones, Trumpet, Mute Trumpet, Synth Leads, Jazz/Gospel Organs
8	Piano	Piano, Electric Piano, Honky Tonk Piano, Harpsichord, Clavi
9	Novelty	Melodic Percussion, Wah Trumpet, Synth, Whistle, Kazoo, Perc. Organ
10	Bellows	Accordion, French Accordion, Mussette, Harmonica, Pump Organ, Bagpipes